Get Out Of Your Own Way

Stop sabotaging your business
and learn to Stand Out in a
crowded market

Lynda Holt

Published by

NABO

NATIONWIDE ALLIANCE OF BUSINESS OWNERS

Get Out Of Your Own Way

Stop sabotaging your business and learn to Stand Out in a crowded market

Get the mindset and skills for success...

Lynda Holt

First published in Great Britain in 2012 by
NABO (UK) Ltd
39-43 Putney High Street
Putney
London
SW15 1SP
Tel: 0208 788 9064
www.nabo.biz

Cover design by Mauve Design Limited, Sutton Coldfield

Typeset by ALS Designs, Waterlooville, Hampshire.

ISBN 978-0-9566192-3-5

Printed and bound in Great Britain by
CPI Antony Rowe, Chippenham.

British Library Cataloguing in Publication Data.

Contents

List of figures, tables and boxes

Figures

Tables

Boxes

List of case studies and exercises

Case studies

Exercises

Acknowledgements

Success is rarely down to one person and I'd like to thank the following people for their help, support and inspiration in the creation of this book.

William Dolan   Richard Oppenheimer

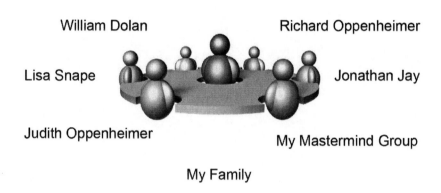

Lisa Snape   Jonathan Jay

Judith Oppenheimer   My Mastermind Group

My Family

I'd also like to thank the many great people - role models, mentors, friends and clients, who've influenced my thinking, supported me on my journey, tested out my ideas and given me a push when I've needed it.

About Lynda

Having sat and thought about what you might actually want to know about me, I decided the following; you want to know what gives me the credibility to write this book, what am I like, whether you would trust me, if you believe I am authentic - do I really do the stuff, or do I just talk about it? Most of all, you want to know what will you get from spending your time reading this book and how will it help you with your dreams and goals.

So to answer your questions, here's a bit about my story, not the corporate road map; the bits that matter to me, the things that might make a difference to you.

I started my business nearly 12 years ago, and from the beginning it was based on my most precious values; freedom and authenticity. To start with freedom was about my own lifestyle; now it has become an important part of what I do with clients, creating businesses that set you free. The authenticity is about me living my dream, being me, using my skills in ways that I enjoy; ways that genuinely benefit those I work with and allow my business to grow in directions I want it to. What I've learned, and share evangelically, is that we are most successful when true to ourselves, not when we are trying to be what others want, or trying to fit into a role or job that constraints us.

The thing is, I love people and my real satisfaction comes out of helping them to see that they can do, or be, whatever it is that's important to them. This is often about self-belief, drive and passion not just skill, resources, and contacts - although these do help enormously. Over the years I've molded my business to suit my passions and strengths and things I really enjoy doing.

I love new challenges - growing and developing projects as well as people - so I've combined the two. First, by changing my health care consultancy into a development consultancy – still in the health sector, and then by adding 360° feedback to my toolkit to support the leadership and cultural development work I do. This quickly grew, with colleagues, old clients and other coaches asking how they could get hold of this 360 thing. In fact the 360° feedback brings clients to me - I don't have to go looking for them. That is a result of niche positioning and product, something any of us can achieve with some thought, effort and focused action.

Even better, the model opened the door to a new venture, allowing me to stretch my entrepreneurial muscles. I partnered up with Appraisal360 and developed the Appraisal360 Practitioner Network and over the last two years have worked with some fabulous coaches and consultants, developing their businesses by applying the principles in this book. Where many great coaches and consultants struggle is on the business skill set - the things that make you stand out and get clients coming to you. This is what I teach through the 360 Profit Programmes. I am very proud that we have created business development packages that are about both mindset and skill set.

I have a long record of supporting others to identify, work towards and achieve their dream, passion and potential. I will challenge you, question you, mentor you and help you implement strategies I have used successfully in my own business. That's what I'm passionate about and where you will benefit the most.

In my 15 years in the NHS I grew from staff nurse to nurse specialist in emergency care, to senior management and held national strategic positions. In all of these roles it was the impact and influence on those I worked with - the team, the patients, other agencies - that created the real successes.

I have always had a passion for continued learning, so I constantly push myself, learn with the best, consolidate and test out and apply what I learn. I have some great mentors and role models.

I am a Trustee of the Centaurus Trust, which enables children with autism, as well as other disabled / disadvantaged children and young people, to enjoy equine facilitated learning, horse boy camps and expand their communication and interaction with others through their contact with the horses.

For those of you who want the credentials, I have qualifications in Corporate and Personal Coaching (CA), Neuro-linguistic Programming (INLPTA) and hypnosis, as well as in leadership and management and in adult education, a master's degree in Medical Sociology and a DipHE in Health Science, and I am a Registered Nurse with specialist qualifications in emergency care. I am a Fellow of the Institute of Leadership and Management and a member of European Mentoring and Coaching Council and of the International Coach Federation.

I hope you like my story and **more importantly**, I hope it makes you think about your story; who you are, what you want, and whether you are running your own life and business in the way you want to.

Enjoy reading this book.

Introduction

People don't fail in business because they lack the technical skills of their trade: they fail because of a combination of inner-game and business-skill challenges. Those in the 'people development' industry are no different. Good coaches struggle to make a living from their coaching practice, consultants consistently get caught in a time-for-money trap and many good trainers spend time chasing work. In this book I intend to explore some of the behaviours, beliefs and actions that lead to success and apply them to creating a 360° feedback product as part of your business offering.

When I use the term 'coach' in this book I'm referring to coaches, consultants, learning and development (L&D) professionals and trainers who collectively form part of the 'people development' industry. The challenges we face are similar, regardless of which specific facet of people development we belong to. One of those challenges is the sheer size of the market, the number of potential clients, and the number of potential suppliers. So a key issue is about learning to stand out from the crowd. This book will look at the business strategies you need to stand out and it will give you a formula for successful niching, and developing your expert status in your chosen area. The book will also address some of the sabotaging behaviours coaches engage in that prevent them from standing out in a crowded market.

Attitude and behaviour are key indicators of success, and not just in business, so I will be sharing the Seven Steps to a Success Mindset, a formula modelled on the behaviours of successful people. To make this work for you, the book will also explore strategies to help you 'get out of your own way'.

Having a product to sell gives you access to a wider customer base and enables you to become visible to anyone looking for that specific product, rather than just to those who know you or of you. The product you choose should be well understood in the industry and have a wide potential customer base. One of the potentially sabotaging behaviours 'people developers' commonly engage in, is developing cleverly named products that mean nothing to their potential clients until they are explained. This is not a reflection on the products themselves – most that I have seen are extremely good – it is a reflection on their marketability. Having 'tools' in your toolkit that are commonly used in the industry, ones with known value and understood outcomes – such as psychometric tools or 360° feedback – increases your marketability and credibility with potential clients.

Part 2 of the book will introduce the skill set you need for a successful business. Chapters 9 – 13 will take you through your business critically examining where you are and where you want to go. It is designed to make you stop and think, it may well identify some blind spots about your business and client group, and it will give you a strategy for achieving your business goals.

Chapters 13, 14 and 15 explain how to use 360° feedback as part of your toolkit. You will learn how to create 360 questionnaires for your target market, how to build on your niche value by using them, and how to use 360° feedback to gain access to potential clients whom you might not otherwise have encountered. The book also covers the practical aspects of setting up and running a good 360° feedback project and, critically, how to generate further business at the end of the project.

Selling is often a challenge for coaches. The reasons for this and some of the limiting beliefs that make selling incredibly hard for some of us are explored in Chapters 16 and 17. The methods that successful people use to sell, including many in our own industry, will be discussed and I will share a formula for conducting a successful sales meeting. One of the potentially sabotaging mistakes that many coaches and consultants still make is to focus on what their service or product can give to the potential client rather than on the outcome for the client, which should reflect the direct answer to the client's problem. These two chapters consider how to identify specific problems, the values behind the issues and how to present a compelling outcome for the potential client if they do business with you.

In short, this book will help you get the business you want, it will show you how to use a product or service to attract the clients you want, using 360° feedback as a model, and it will make you stop and think about how you impact on your business success now. I am really looking forward to taking you on a journey through your business, ensuring you have the mindset strategies, the market positioning skills and the sales techniques to accelerate your success.

PART 1

Your Success Mindset

Part 1 explores the Seven Steps to a Success Mindset. It focuses on how you impact on your business success, for better and for worse. The section highlights some of the beliefs and behaviours that inadvertently sabotage your success. Using the Seven Steps to a Success Mindset, it then identifies how to prime yourself for success instead.

CHAPTER 1
Seven Steps to a
Success Mindset

This section explores the Seven Steps to a Success Mindset. Each step layers on the previous one to make you unstoppable.

Box 1.1: Seven Steps to a Success Mindset

1. Take responsibility for your own mind.
2. Build your business on passion and purpose.
3. Dream big and set clear goals to make your dream happen.
4. Create a plan and take action.
5. Apply personal excellence to everything.
6. Maintain persistent focus.
7. Invest in yourself.

These Seven Steps, together with continual action towards your dream, are the recipe for personal success. This part of the book will ensure that you have the right ingredients going into your bowl. The Seven Steps have been derived by modelling the behaviours of successful business people, some famous like Richard Branson and Anita Roddick, and some known to me personally as colleagues and mentors.

This is the bit that, in the people development business, we think we already know; and for the most part we do – the theory at least. Like many other professional groups, coaches are often very poor at applying their own industry knowledge to themselves. Hence we see many very good and even excellent coaches failing in business. Their own mindsets get in the way of their success. So before moving on to the business skills required for success, let's examine and apply the powerful mindset strategies you need for success.

Evidence and examples present themselves time and time again; people get what they expect in life. Our mindsets, the unconscious patterns we run and our beliefs around specific issues, determine how we behave, how we present ourselves to others and, ultimately, the results we get from any given situation. Put bluntly:

"We get what we expect."

How we communicate with ourselves is even more important than how we communicate with our potential clients. It is your internal communication that sets the parameters for your mind. Both the language you use on yourself and the extent to which you allow your imagination to create your future, good and bad, has a direct impact on the limits you create for yourself and your ability to move yourself and others to take action.

Taking charge of your mind

Any changes in the way you run your business start in your mind. Sometimes the decision is an unconscious one based on an experience; sometimes it is an active one to do something differently, reinforced by the perceived benefit. Your business is where it is as a direct result of what is going on in your mind. You may argue that this is not the only factor, and often this is true, but you can be sure that it is almost always part of the picture. Where you are has a direct result on where you let your imagination take you. And what you imagine has a direct impact on your mood or emotional state, your physiology and therefore what you project.

One of our first challenges in creating a Success Mindset is to manage our internal communication, and subsequently what we allow ourselves to imagine. This is necessary to prevent the creation of habit-forming failure spirals. I will give you an example of a great failure spiral of my own creation, something that damaged my business, something that affected my performance and something that I had manufactured in my own imagination.

A few years ago, when Health Service 360 was a relatively new brand, I was asked to pitch for some business with a fairly large NHS organisation. The project included providing a 360° feedback intervention for the organisation's team of senior medical consultants and the primary focus of the intervention was on developing their leadership skills. Better still, there was potential for further work, providing leadership development and coaching, at the end of the 360 process. So, having had a number of discussions with the HR director, submitted a written proposal and been shortlisted as one of the final two suppliers, I was invited to attend an interview with the HR director, medical director and CEO.

That was where my problems started. I immediately focused on who the other company would be and I decided that it must be a specific competitor as they had the biggest share of the market. My failure spiral then began to become a self-fulfilling prophecy. I started to think that my competitor was more experienced, that they had more client stories to draw on and that they had more credibility because most of their team were men in their late 40s and early 50s who best matched the group of doctors that we were targeting.

My confidence waivered; I started to see where I was not as good; I started to imagine things going badly and the client not taking me as seriously as my competitor. Psychologically, I started to prepare for failure, to convince myself, even, that this was not the right project, and to accept that the experience of presenting was an end in itself. So by the time I got to the meeting, and as I sat outside the room waiting for my turn, I was nervous, unsure of how my product stacked up against that of my competitor, and I had even convinced myself that my image was wrong for the client. Guess what? I did a lousy pitch and I didn't get the business. Exactly what I'd expected, planned for and conditioned myself to do.

The irony was that I actually had a much better leadership 360 than my competitor. I could provide the coaching and leadership development that my competitor could not – they just provided 360° feedback for doctors. I was more credible in that I am a clinician, I have spent 15 years working in the NHS and speak the same niche linguistics. The real sting came a week or so later when the HR director rang me to ask what had happened. He told me we had been the preferred supplier until the presentations. During the meeting the medical director had decided, based on my performance, there was no chance of me managing the consultants' reactions and behaviours, and so I lost the project.

I had created a whole load of sabotages based completely on my fabricated imagination. Imagine how the pitch would have gone if I'd been running the script from the paragraph above instead.

When we worry about what might happen, or about what people think of us, or about what we believe about our own potential, we can very quickly manifest a failure spiral (Figure 1.1).

Figure 1.1 - Failure Spiral

Self-limiting belief

Imagine things going badly

Plan for failure

Consequences

project anxiety
& uncertainty

Self-fulfilling prophecy

The key is to be consciously aware of how and where you focus attention, because just as this spiral can lead to failure, it can also lead to success. Allowing your imagination and inner talk to take you toward your dream is just as effective. From here, you can instead create beliefs that support you, prepare for success and create the emotions, mood and physiology associated with achieving your dream. This will instantaneously change what you project to the world.

What you pay attention to is critical because this is where your focus lies. Where your focus lies is where your effort and energy goes. So paying attention to what you don't want is a great way to create a failure spiral and to end up with exactly what you didn't want.

You are 100% responsible for your own attitude, actions and results. This doesn't mean you should be happy and positive 100% of the time and never react to what life throws at you – unless you choose to be that way. It does, however, mean that your outer experience of the world is a direct result of your inner perceptions.

If you are not getting what you want out of your business it is likely that some self-limiting belief or 'boundary condition' is holding you back. In personal development terms, a boundary condition is the limit of your conscious knowledge, or the edge of what you think you really know. To put it differently, it is the limit of your comfort zone. The self-belief that keeps you safe can also stop from you going beyond what you already know.

> ## "We are boxed in by the boundary conditions of our own thinking."
>
> Albert Einstein

Undoubtedly your habits and self-limiting behaviours can create an invisible wall inside which you operate. This, in effect, will sabotage your business.

As you work through the Seven Steps to a Success Mindset, instead of thinking 'I'm a coach, I know this stuff', choose to consider how you may be sabotaging your own success. What limiting beliefs or boundary conditions are you carrying? Most of all, remember that only you can change your thinking. What you focus on is an active choice – if you choose to make it.

CHAPTER 2

Step 1: Take responsibility for your own mind

Taking responsibility for your own mind is largely about taking control of your beliefs, values and habits. Your attitude really is the difference between a Success Mindset, which sets you free, and a mindset that holds you back.

Ninety per cent of our thoughts occur at an unconscious level. This is where your inner beliefs and self-talk really begin to influence your outer projections. Therefore, not surprisingly, our biggest successes and greatest satisfaction come when actions and behaviour are congruent with our inner self, our values and beliefs. This does not mean that you should adopt the position some business owners take, which is 'I am who I am, so I'm not changing'. This is business sabotage.

What congruence does mean is that when your conscious mind and actions are in sync with your unconscious beliefs and values you are at your most powerful. It is therefore in your interests to understand those circumstances where they may not be congruent. When your conscious intent or action and unconscious beliefs are different, you lack conviction and feel robbed of energy, direction, power and focus. As a result even simple tasks can seem hard and unrewarding.

Imagine yourself as both navigator (your conscious mind) and driver (your unconscious mind) of your life. You get in the car and set off. You both know where you want to go, but there the difficulty starts: the navigator says 'Turn left' and the driver sees a narrow road with lots of bumps and obstacles. While thinking about whether or not he can handle the bumpy road the driver misses the turning and, not believing the navigator's direction, insists that there must be an easier road. The driver then struggles to find a place where he can turn round and becomes less confident in taking the navigator's direction. Before they know what has happened, both the driver and the navigator are some way off the course they had embarked upon and further away from where they wanted to be.

If you let your beliefs and values drive your life, as most people do, be sure that they are values and beliefs that support and empower you, not ones that constrain you. So as far as seeking congruence is concerned, work on yourself first. Identify beliefs that don't serve you, and take responsibility for them.

One of the main reasons people don't take action to achieve their goals is that they don't take responsibility for themselves. They believe success to be outside of their control and they make excuses for themselves and blame external influences – therefore letting go of their own power.

One of the quickest ways to take control of your mindset is to stop being a victim. Everybody behaves like a victim occasionally and that's probably OK, although unhelpful. It's when you live in victimhood that it becomes a problem. It's easy to find such a person: nothing is their fault, their life is harder than anyone else's, their luck is worse, and there is always someone or something else to blame. Victims feed off others' sympathy and things going wrong. Not a good way to run a business!

As a coach, you will know when you are being a victim – but in case you don't see it in yourself, Box 2.1 offers some clues.

Box 2.1: I am a victim because...

- I always get bad luck
- I would have got the client but ...
- It always goes wrong for me
- This stuff doesn't happen to anyone else
- It isn't easy for me because ...
- I work really hard but success is out of my control
- Other people have more fun
- Other people get more help
- Other people have it easier than me

It's easy to favour victimhood because it saves you from having to take action, from moving out of your comfort zone, and, most of all, ensures that nothing is actually your fault. In order to take control of your mindset and operate from a position of power you need to understand your own beliefs and values, where they come from and whether or not they serve you well.

The most common areas to look in terms of business success are based around the views you hold about yourself and your ability, and your attitudes to wealth and success. A good place to start is with what you believe to be true. This will help you to identify which beliefs are narrow and restrict your life and which beliefs are transforming and expand your potential.

Many limiting beliefs come from other people's imprint or the boundary conditions discussed earlier. These are based on your experiences to date and, most critically, your perceptions of those experiences. Left unexamined, these imprints and boundary conditions determine how you feel, the way you behave and what level of risk you are prepared to take.

Case study 1: Limiting beliefs

Rosemary, a client of mine, who is married with a grown up son, has a coaching business, and works with senior managers to improve their leadership skills. She came to me first because she wanted to use 360° feedback to attract more clients. When we examined her business, which was about five years old, she worked mostly with the same organisations who regularly re-employed her for other projects, so she obviously delivered value. She charged by the hour and used the same flat rate for all clients.

When we explored why she wanted to get more clients she said her business wasn't really making money. It had always yielded about £15,000 p.a. and she wanted to make more. Further exploration revealed she was qualified in a whole range of psychometrics none of which she used with clients. I felt sure the 360° feedback would be the same and that something else was responsible for Rosemary's financial plateau.

You see, Rosemary had a whole range of limiting beliefs about money - where it should come from in the family and, most importantly, that she couldn't out earn her husband. Why? Because Rosemary's own parents had divorced when she was young and she lost touch with her father. Her mother had persistently told her it was because she had earned more than her husband. Rosemary, therefore, established a boundary condition for herself that stopped her from out earning her own husband.

Rosemary's perception was not based on any reality and had limited her business growth, it stopped her from using her skills and from charging what she was worth. Some discussions with her husband and an adjustment of perception enabled Rosemary to change her attitude and make different choices. Not surprisingly, Rosemary's revenue began to increase, she attracted different clients, and is much more satisfied with her business.

Identifying potentially limiting beliefs about money and success gives you an opportunity to change them, should you choose to do so. Beliefs that sabotage success fall into three broad categories. Here are a few to get you thinking:

1. Negative money beliefs such as:

   - Money is evil.
   - Rich people are greedy/dishonest.
   - Money is difficult to get.
   - There's a limit to how much I can earn.
   - I can only earn more by working harder.
   - Money is more quickly spent than earned.

2. Identity and self-belief

   - I don't deserve money.
   - I'm not good enough to make money.
   - If I'm successful, my friends will be jealous and stop liking me.
   - I may just forget what's truly important and not like the person I've become.

- I can't charge that much.
- I don't have unique talents or abilities.
- I will never have enough.
- I'm never lucky.

3. Value beliefs

- The more money I have, the more problems I will have.
- It's impossible to have it all: a loving family, a job I love, great friends, good health and lots of money.
- Life is meant to be a struggle.
- Only dreamers think they can get rich, but I'm a realist.
- It's OK to be able to survive each day.
- It's more important to be liked for who I am than because I am rich.

Exercise 1: Examining beliefs

Your current beliefs around money, wealth and success warrant some examination, so ask yourself:

1. What stories were told in my family about money?
2. What messages have I got from others?
3. What judgements and generalisations do I make as a result?
4. What meaning do I attach to wealth?
5. What difficult feelings do I experience about money now?
6. What do I feel about success and where does money fit in?

When you look at your answers to the above what do they tell you?

How do they impact on your current experience of success and wealth?

Are you happy with this?

Do these 'truths' empower you or limit you?

If your current beliefs about money and success don't serve you and you are not getting the results you want, choose some new ones.

To do this, first take responsibility for where you are now and how successful your business is today. Accept that you are the cause of your current situation and it's not the effect of circumstances. When you accept this, it's much easier to take charge of your actions and your results. Accepting responsibility allows you to really consider the validity of your perceptions and make a change if you want to. This is your place of power. A small shift in perception about a belief or value can significantly change your reactions and your behaviour, and therefore the outcome you get.

For example, a man who believes that rich people are dishonest is limiting himself from becoming rich, if he values honesty. In order to attract wealth, he needs a perception shift. Examining where his belief comes from, whether it is really true in his life now and whether it is a useful belief to hold on to will allow him to make a choice about how he sees rich people from now on. If he chooses to change his perception he will become more congruent with becoming rich himself, and the work of achieving riches will become easier.

In order to achieve a change in perception it is first necessary to understand what it is that you want to change, and this comes from self-awareness, from understanding what, specifically, you are thinking and doing that is getting in the way. Once you have identified this it will be easier to find a different way of thinking. If, for example, you dislike networking, you probably have a list of reasons why it doesn't work and therefore hold a belief that it's a waste of time; so when you go along to a networking meeting this will be what you subconsciously seek to reinforce, what you project and, most likely, what you get. Your challenge is to determine whether your belief serves you and, if not, what would help you achieve a better outcome. Perhaps networking is a good place to build relationships.

Thinking differently is the first step to embedding a different belief. Of course it's not as easy as simply saying: 'From now on, I think networking is a good place to build relationships'. This new thought pattern needs to be reinforced many times over before it becomes the default neuro-pathway. For many people, mantras or affirmations help. Having the affirmation written down somewhere you will see it is beneficial, as is making time to remind yourself of your new perception. Bill Clinton very famously used the mantra 'It's the economy, stupid', to keep himself and his team on message during the 1992 US presidential election campaign; in fact, it hung on the wall in his office. Positive affirmations alone are not enough; time and effort has to go into reprogramming your brain.

Doing something different helps to support your ability to think something different. Even a small change to your normal routine around the belief you want to change can make a big difference to the perceptions you hold and the perceptions you create. So, to use our networking example, a small change in the way you behave – maybe arriving earlier, introducing yourself to someone you don't know, rather than looking for someone you do know, or waiting for someone to talk to you – will give you a different perspective. If you have gone to the meeting to build relationships, as opposed to wasting your time, you are likely to have far more useful conversations with people.

Achieving a mindset change may also involve reviewing the company you keep. It's important to know who has contributed to your old beliefs and will, inadvertently, seek to reinforce them. It may be that you need to protect yourself from these people while you are embedding your new belief; and at the very least you should be consciously aware that you don't need to absorb their perception. For example, the friend you go to network meetings with - the one who also thinks they are a waste of time, but at least the two of you get time to catch up - is perhaps not the person to accompany you to meetings during your transition. In fact, it is often conversation and time spent with new people whose views differ from yours, that widens your perspective and helps to create the perception shifts that help you grow.

Finally, the most important aspect of achieving a perception shift is to make sure that you take some action to get out of your comfort zone.

"Until you make the unconscious conscious, it will direct your life and you will call it fate."

Carl Jung

CHAPTER 3

Step 2: Build your business on passion and purpose

One of the big things with words and phrases like 'passion', 'follow your passion', etc. is that everyone's interpretation of the meaning is slightly different. So to be clear, in this book when I talk about 'passion' I mean the things you want to do, that you find easy and natural; the things that you enjoy talking about and learning about; those things that you do or would do even if you weren't getting paid. 'Purpose' is why you do it: your deeply held values and drivers, and the reason why your passion matters to you.

Building a successful business takes hard work and effort. If you are following someone else's dream or passion, doing what you think you should do, or what seems the safe or sensible thing, it's unlikely that you are following your true passion. Here are some depressing facts about owning your own business: depending what you read, up to 50% of new businesses fail in the first year, and fewer than 10% of businesses will be around after 10 years. It's fair to say that there are many reasons why small businesses cease trading. Often it's down to financial pressure; and also people find the business-owner life-style is not what they want, or they quite simply lose their nerve, decide it's not working and go back into a job.

For businesses that survive the first couple of years (the concept and development phase), a further significant proportion – up to 40% of remaining businesses – cease trading in years 2 to 4. This is where the lack of passion in your business really gets you: the novelty has worn off, the challenge of develop or abort has gone, and what is left is maintaining sustainable activity and routine tasks. Without fire and passion for your business, it's difficult to keep growing, to create the following, the demand and the excitement that engages new clients and ultimately gives you a successful business.

It is at this stage that average business owners and real entrepreneurs really start to divide. Many people find a level in business at which they are comfortable or solvent, and then seek to sustain it. Passion sets the average business owner aside from the really inspiring business leaders. All of these business stars or leaders are passionate about what they do, how they do it and their product or company.

> Take Tony Robbins, for example. As a young man he wanted to help people; he's made it a life-long crusade and he's become very wealthy by following his passion. It's his passion that sets him aside from any other NLP practitioners. Love or hate his style, no one can deny the energy and passion that goes into his presentations, his products and his brand. It's that very energy and passion that gets him the followers, the clients and the success he now enjoys. He lives his own passion.

Passionate entrepreneurs learn how to trust their gut and follow their instincts; they don't live in a world of 'should dos', and they don't expect to get it right every time. They know that what they're doing matters, it makes a difference; and therefore when the going gets tough, as it always does at some point in your business, they have the drive and the motivation to keep going.

"Happiness and success in life are not the result of what we have, but rather how we live"

Anthony Robbins

This is driven by purpose, the reasons you are passionate about what you do. These reasons vary from person to person: the things that drive one won't necessarily drive another, so it's important to understand your values and their congruence with your business.

Money is rarely the real purpose behind a business: it might be one of the desired outcomes, but is not commonly why successful business leaders do what they do. The money trap motivates and demotivates in equal measure. The money cycle can very easily become the money trap. You set off wanting money – you get it, you spend it – you want more – you get it, you spend it – and so on, until it becomes unsustainable. When the going gets tough, people in this cycle often look for a better or faster way to make money – they don't stick with a business.

If you think the primary purpose you started your business was to make money (as opposed to making money being an outcome), ask yourself why you do what you're doing, and keep asking until you've exhausted the reasons. If you can't find reasons other than money, check that you're working in an area you are truly passionate about.

Case study 2: Passion for your business

Frank worked in the finance industry, he came to see me because he couldn't see how his new consultancy business was ever going to make the sort of money he'd been making in the banking industry. To be honest neither could I. However, there must have been a reason why Frank had decided to start his own business. To begin with he said it was because he could make more money. Our first exercise was to identify what the drivers for starting his business were, i.e. his purpose. Frank said that there were a number of high-paying clients who he knew would pay him for advice, rather than the company he had worked for. So he believed he would make money from his new business.

Frank also described feeling drained and burnt out in his job. He felt he had more to offer people by teaching them about their money and investments rather than by managing things for them. This was quite a change from his previous job, and the clients he'd started with didn't all stick around – some wanted their investments managed for them, as Frank had been doing before.

When he left his job Frank didn't really know what he was passionate about; he just knew that it wasn't that job anymore. We explored what he had enjoyed about his job to identify his drivers and revealed he loved the buzz, the challenge of finding the best deal, acting quickly and getting better results for his clients than others did for theirs. We discussed the sort of money he was handling and the commissions he made. He realized that really that wasn't his passion either. That's when Frank's breakthrough came – he'd always believed making money was his driver, the thing that motivated him most; it wasn't. To use his words, it was knowing he'd got the absolute best for his client, the thrill of the chase, and that he'd used his skill to better their lives. The fact he got paid well for it was secondary.

So, having identified some drivers, or purpose, in his old job, how did that translate to Frank's new business? The business he had created allowed him to use all the same skills to better his clients' lives and to help them become the best they could be at managing their own money and investments. Frank really believed that his clients could get more from less, financially, if they knew what they were doing. This was the message he wanted to share; this was his passion.

Passion and purpose identified, we revisited money. How could Frank make the sort of money he'd made in his previous job? He said that he didn't really believe he could at this stage, but it didn't matter now, he didn't actually need the sort of money he'd been making in order to sustain his lifestyle. In fact Frank wasn't really sure that he needed to work at all from a purely financial point of view because he managed his own investments well. That was a couple of years ago. His business is doing really well and he continues to enjoy the buzz and the challenge of using his expertise to benefit his clients.

When you're passionate about your business and you understand your purpose, things flow; passion is contagious and people are attracted to your energy and enthusiasm. This doesn't mean that if you don't feel passionate about your business right now, you're in the wrong business. It just means you may have some work to do on your mindset. In my Success Mindset programme we spend at least a day ensuring that we really understand what your passions are and why you started your business. In the everyday running of your business it's not uncommon to lose sight of why you do what you do and why it's important to you. Once the excitement of setting up the business wears off and the reality of the routine stuff you need to do to actually sustain the business becomes apparent, it can be easy to lose direction, to get bogged down in the business, to stop being creative and to stop forward moving. Having a business based on your passions doesn't mean that you won't have to work hard, but it does help you to stay focused – and for the most part you can be working on what you love.

> *"A business has to be involving, it has to be fun, and it has to exercise your creative instincts."*

Richard Branson

Identifying your passion

Many of us have a clear passion when we start out, and that's a great start. It doesn't mean you should leap in blindly. You still need to be sure that it's not something you enjoy as a hobby but don't have the desire to do all the time. Even more importantly, your business idea has to be marketable; it has to have something that people want and are prepared to pay for. This will be covered in more detail the niching section of this book.

If you don't think you have a business based on your passions, or have no clue what you are passionate about, this section should help you. Not knowing your passion should not be seen as a block to developing or setting up your business. You are surrounded by endless possibilities – the only limit is your own imagination. This is about the ideas you have and your reaction to them. It is also about your perception of what a passionate person is and how that fits with your values. Passionate people don't all behave in the same way, yet many of us carry around stereotypes of what 'passionate' looks like – and then make a load of value judgements about whether or not we fit the profile.

Everyone has the right to be passionate about what excites them; we all have multiple purposes that drive us, ones that we believe in absolutely; and we all express our passion differently.

Box 3.1: Eight steps to identifying your passion

1. Give yourself permission.
2. Explore possibilities.
3. Look at what you already do.
4. Ask yourself some powerful questions.
5. Get creative.
6. Test it.
7. Look for fulfilment.
8. Make it happen.

Give yourself permission

The most critical step in finding your passion is to give yourself permission to be passionate. If your own beliefs about passion are getting in your way, go back to Step 1 and repeat Exercise 1 – this time about passion.

Explore possibilities

Many people get stuck finding their passion because they believe it focuses on one absolute. This is rarely the case. Passion is a spectrum, with things we love doing at one end and things we hate doing at the other (Figure 3.1).

Figure 3.1 The Passion Spectrum

Things I love to do — Like — Dislike — Things I hate to do

If you don't know what you love doing, start with what you like. Base your business on the 'Like' end of the spectrum and then work towards what you love. Explore different things that you like. Spend some time playing with your options and let your imagination help you to find your passion.

Look at what you already do

Often what we love is right under our noses – we just may not have thought about it as a business, or we may believe that we can't make money out of it. Do you know what is under your nose?

- What do you learn about for fun?
- What inspires you?
- What do you research when online?
- What can you talk about for hours, until you lose track of time?
- What section do you go to first in a bookshop?
- What makes you feel alive, interested, fired up?

Ask yourself some powerful questions

Make the time to invest in yourself and your passion – and get some help if you need to. Look at your answers to the questions above and ask yourself the following:

- What would I do even if I didn't get paid for it?
- What is my gift to the world?
- What do I find easy?
- When are the times that I feel most creative?
- What examples are there of great things I've done?

Just scribble down whatever comes to mind, and keep scribbling until you have nothing else to say. Then go through your lists, looking for trends and themes. What you like, or even love, and what you are most interested in and most successful at should begin to emerge now.

Get creative

Look at what is emerging and start to create your ideal business or develop your existing business along the lines of your passion. Explore all the possibilities, even if your ideal business doesn't exist yet, think about creating it.

> James Dyson has a great passion for inventing things. When he became frustrated with the poor suction of the vacuum cleaner he decided to make something better. When he started work on the bagless vacuum cleaner it reportedly took five years and 5,126 prototypes before he came up with the Dyson vacuum cleaner. He is now worth somewhere in the region of $2 billion. His passion for creating things drove him to this.

If you consider our own industry, there are always opportunities to fill a gap in the market. The challenge is to ensure that you fill it with something people want. My own business is a good example of this. My passions are very much about growth and potential and I'm very lucky to have created a business that allows me to work with what I'm passionate about every day. This is because I found a gap – no, a gaping hole – in my industry. In the 360° feedback world many companies teach technical skill in using 360° feedback, and that's where they stop. Others teach the business and marketing skills desperately needed by many in the people development industry, and for the most part yet another group teach the powerful mindset strategies. I have created a business that pulls together the mindset and the skill set in one place. This enables me to walk my clients through a process of personal growth and business development and gives them niche products so they can start earning in their business as soon as they are ready. I exploited that gap because it allows me to bundle together the things I love doing and am good at; it enables me to give my clients something that really makes a difference to their lives and their businesses. Why? Because that is what I value: being part of their journey to success, knowing that my coaching or teaching has in some way moved them closer to their potential. When I look back on my career, this has always been one of my drivers, even in my NHS days, when that was not my 'job'.

Being creative is about taking what you love doing and finding a way to use it to make a difference to others, a difference that they will pay for. Then you have a business based on passion.

Test it

When you think you've found your passion, test it out before putting all your eggs in one basket. Are you still reading about it after the first couple of books? Try a class. Do you enjoy being with like-minded people? Talk to people who are doing what you want to do. If you are still interested, test your passion out as a business. This can be done very cheaply with the aid of a bit of online marketing and a few contacts, it is not wise at this stage to spend large amounts on business collateral and authority websites. If you're still interested and enjoying your passion after a few months and you have a few customers, then you can start to build from basics.

Look for fulfilment

To remain successful and rewarding in the long term, your business must align with your values. There are no right or wrong values: it's a question of fulfilling your purpose for being in business. It simply means that you need to be making a difference to your clients in a way that matters to you. It doesn't mean you have to be famous or to make millions – unless, of course, that is what you want.

Make it happen

To build a business on passion and purpose, you need to take real action, not play at it. Succeeding in business is not a hobby. Making things happen takes commitment, purpose and passion, and a business area – be it a product or service or both – that you are prepared to commit to, that has potential for expansion and that is in demand.

Passion for your business makes success easier; it engages people and excites them. Mix with other passionate people and learn to be comfortable with your passions and the purpose behind them.

CHAPTER 4

Step 3: Dream big and set clear goals to make your dream happen

In the people development industry goals are big business. We work with our clients' goals and organisational goals; we're paid to facilitate goal setting and goal achievement; and most of us know several goal-setting models inside out. My experience of working with coaches on their own businesses is twofold: first, we are less good at applying some of these principles to ourselves and our own businesses; and second, we are less familiar with some of the theory of how goals work than we are with the models.

"Imagination is everything. It is the preview of life's coming attractions."

Albert Einstein

Rather than discussing how you set goals for your business, which you probably know already, this chapter will consider why goals are part of the Success Mindset and how they help you to realise your dream.

How well developed is your dream? Is it big, wild and not quite within touching distance? It should be. When you think about it, if you have a Success Mindset, work in your passion and work with purpose, playing a small game is unlikely to be very satisfying. Your real, true passion and your dream for your business – the secret one, the one you might be too embarrassed to share – may seem outright ridiculous from where you're looking now. If it isn't, it possibly isn't big enough – a life dream isn't usually something you can reach in one go.

The dream part of the process is what you want for your business, what you want your life to be like – maybe how you want to be remembered. Your dream is not about what you need to do. Think of the Wright Brothers – they're remembered as the first men to fly, not for producing the first fixed-wing aircraft that worked.

Be proud of your dream. Make sure that it's not based on your past, or even your present, but on your future, on what you want. Release your entrepreneurial mind, shatter your boundary conditions – the conditions that have constrained you in the past – and dream as if you can have anything in the world. This is when you really start to get fantastic results. Playing small or conservatively in business doesn't get big results. It might maintain the status quo; but if you want more, you have to start dreaming – you know, in the outrageous way we did as children.

Exercise 2: Strategic visioning

Dream big!

Create your vivid picture of success: use your imagination to carve your destiny, the reality you want for your future. Spend time on this, because it is from here that your path is shaped and your goals are set. Know what it looks like, how it smells and what it sounds like. Form some real clarity about how you feel here, about the emotions associated with your dream.

In whatever way works best for you, get your dream down – on paper, in a book, on a vision board – write, draw, scribble. Make it as detailed as possible.

Remember, this is your dream, not your goals. You don't need to write anything in goal-setting formats, i.e. set in the present, time-frames, etc. You do need to be sure that your dream consists of what you do want, not what you don't want. For example, you may dream of a future of wealth and abundance (with all the specifics of what this means to you, of course). This is very different from a future where you don't want to be - in debt. Your dream is your focus, your passion, so it must be something you can believe in and buy into as your reality.

Once you have your dream, it's much easier to start on goals. There is much debate about goals and goal setting – whether big goals work or small, achievable goals are better, or even whether goal setting works at all. To some extent it depends on the individual and the way in which goals are being used. A word of caution though: the wrong goals can seriously mess up your dream.

Case study 3: Make your goals support your dream

Jane was a single mum who wanted to be financially secure and have time to spend with her two young children. Her dream was to 'be there' for her children, give them the experiences she wanted them to have and live a life of abundance and adventure, as well as to build a business in an area of coaching about which she was passionate: surviving break-up.

Jane came to see me one afternoon, saying that she needed to find a job. This bold statement took me a little by surprise. Nine months before, she had set up a life coaching business near her home and she'd always seemed very committed to her vision.

I asked Jane 'Why?' She said that she'd done her homework, she knew her conversion rates and was achieving her business goal. The results, the work that she needed to put in, meant that her children had to go to a child minder, and this was eating into the financial reward. Jane had concluded that she would have more time with her children and be better off financially in a job.

So what had gone wrong? Jane had created a goal based on how many clients she wanted to generate the money she needed. Her goal was worked out on sound conversion rates – how many free sessions she needed to do in order to get the right number of paying clients. She had then set about finding those people, doing free 30-minute coaching sessions and converting enough people into paying customers; all of which she successfully achieved. Jane's problem was the amount of time she was spending on free coaching sessions, which meant that she was working double hours she wanted to – for no more money. The goal Jane had set and achieved got in the way of her dream – it didn't support it.

Before Jane threw the baby out with the bath water, we looked at what other options she had. It wasn't the paid work that was causing the problem, it was the free stuff – so was all that free coaching necessary? Did Jane need to meet all of her clients face to face? Many had children too and might prefer a different option – except that none had been offered. Equally important, Jane's current model didn't have future scalability; from what I could see she only had the option to trade time for money, and that didn't fit with her dream.

Really, it was no wonder Jane felt tired and frustrated with her business. It jarred with her biggest value – her vision of motherhood. She couldn't see how her model could work and, just as important, it had no potential to deliver the future she was looking for. When I asked her if the concept – the coaching, her niche – was still what she was passionate about, Jane said 'Yes'. I asked if she still believed there was a market for this kind of help; again, she said 'Yes'. Did the purpose of the business still have a place in Jane's dream? Again, the answer was yes.

Jane's a tick-off-the-list sort of person. She thrives on goals and almost always achieves them. We decided she needed a new set of goals, ones that would bring her closer to her dream. Some exploration of options and a review of what others were doing successfully in Jane's niche revealed a whole range of choices. The first was other customer acquisition activities that would remove the need for free coaching. Jane set up an online interview, some 'top tips' to download and an email Q&A. This got her a better conversion rate to paying customer! She's now running an online coaching programme as well as seeing face-to-face clients, and has clients in several countries. Better still, she works while her children are at school and is making just a little more money than in her previous model. This new model also has scalability, when Jane's ready, through its online part.

It's important to ensure that your goals support your dream. If they don't, it's equally important to have the confidence to change them.

Theory behind goals

Goals are designed to be motivating, to provide focus and to target action. They are intrinsically related to needs and values. They work in a kind of hierarchy and are most successful when linked to values.

As humans we have a range of innate needs, things that are necessary for our survival. They are based on our health and well-being, our physical need for things like food and air, and psychological needs for safety, love, etc. We have no real choice when it comes to needs; they exist and we have to find a way to fulfil them. Above needs are our values, which are biologically/psychologically designed to satisfy our needs. Of course, actual values differ from person to person, and they are individually chosen, as discussed in Step 1.

Values can be made into a more or less appealing way of satisfying a need. The actual need doesn't change, but the value changes the way in which a person satisfies that need. For example, you are hungry; any food will reduce or remove the hunger, but you value healthy eating, so rather than reach for any food, you allow your values to control the fulfilment of your need. All of a sudden you don't need just any food to resolve your hunger: you need some fruit. There are many different values that can meet one specific need.

When you layer your goals in life on top of your values, you start to develop a strategy to fulfil your needs by achieving specific things that fit with your objectives and dovetail with your values. For example, if you layer the goal 'I want to lose 10 pounds' on top of the above example, you may come up with 'I want to lose weight so I eat fruit to satisfy my need for food'. These goals are highly individual, so two people with a similar value might have very different goals to meet the same need.

Box 4.1: Goals affect actions

Goals affect actions in three ways:

1. Direct action towards the goal
2. Intensity of effort put into achieving the goal
3. Persistency of effort, particularly in the face of obstacles

---

Goals and motivation have been studied extensively in business, psychology and organisational development. Edwin Locke has studied this over 40 years and has written some of the most seminal work on the subject. In the late 1990s he concluded that in order for a goal to be motivating it needed two key attributes: difficulty and specificity.

Difficulty

Locke further concluded that the more difficult the goal, the higher the performance effort to achieve it. This continued to apply when a goal seemed impossible to fully achieve. This was supported by James C. Collins, the creator of Big Hairy Audacious Goals (BHAG). He believed that grand visions that required sustained effort and promised more pitfalls and problems actually delivered better results than small, easy-to-achieve goals. This is good news for the Success Mindset. It means that big goals, as big as your dream, have a track record of working. What is important here is the steps to success and the markers of achievement along the way are in the goal. This type of goal setting works only where there is a commitment to attaining the outcome, and knowledge or access to the knowledge needed to attain the goal.

Clarity

Locke identified specificity as the second key factor in a goal. The clearer the goal and the more explicit the success markers, the better your performance can be measured against your aim. The greater the specificity of the goal, the less room for ambiguity, for forgetting or changing the markers of achievement, and hence the greater chance of staying on track and achieving the goal. However, it is unlikely that specificity alone will be enough to motivate you to achieve your goal.

Commitment

Another factor affecting goal achievement is commitment. This is best achieved by ensuring that any goal you set for yourself meets both your needs and your values. Research on difficulty shows that commitment to a goal will increase when the goal is more difficult.

Two factors increase commitment:

1. Conviction that the goal is important
2. Confidence that you are capable of making progress and achieving it

Feedback

Essentially, this is the tracking of your performance against the goal you set. The markers of achievement are identified, so you will be able to clearly tell how you are doing. You can identify if you need to focus effort and energy differently to complete the goal, and change strategy if necessary.

Self-efficacy

Self-efficacy differs from self-esteem in that it relates to a specific task or skill set. The idea is based on the work of Albert Bandura in the 1970s. Self-efficacy is a person's belief in his or her ability to succeed in a given situation. This is important, because the greater your self-efficacy in relation to a goal, the stronger your sense of commitment to a goal, the better you are able to problem solve and the better you will be able to recover from setbacks. Self-efficacy increases commitment, resilience and persistence. It is developed through practice, modelling others, being an expert in your topic and through good, old-fashioned self-confidence and inner belief in your abilities.

So how hard should you make your goals?

There are two clear schools of thought: the BHAG model and the Kaizen model. The Kaizen model for goal setting is part of the Japanese system for continuous improvement. This system advocates many small goals, each effecting change, which leads to steady growth and streamlining of activity, both behavioural and functional. For some, this chunked down, small-goal approach can work, particularly when bigger goals seem too intimidating. It allows you to create a series of step goals and can be more flexible. It also reduces the risk of feeling frustrated or that you are failing, if you are not getting close to a big goal quickly enough.

That said, the advantages described in the theory of goals do appear to be much more relevant to BHAG. But big goals can set you up to fail, and the way that you can handle that will, to some extent, determine how you should proceed with goal setting. The bigger the goal, the bigger the perceived failure. This can change the way you feel about your dream, as in the case of Jane, discussed above, who considered giving up on her business and finding a job. It can also leave you disempowered, angry and disappointed, and with a whole lot of other undesirable emotions.

So why is there is an increasing popularity for big, outrageous goals amongst entrepreneurs and successful business owners? In part, it is because the bigger your dream, the more you can achieve and, even more importantly, it is because you choose your attitude to the outcome of your goal. You can choose to feel like a failure because you didn't quite reach your goal, or you can choose to feel like a star because you are so much closer to your goal than you were when you started.

Case study 4: Feeling like a star

Tom wanted to run some 360° feedback seminars for GPs. His goal was to get 30 GPs in a room so that after his presentation he could recruit four more 360 coaching clients. He worked hard to get doctors along to his seminar, and by the time of the event 22 were booked to come. On the evening, 14 showed up. Tom was disappointed because this was just under half of his target. In that moment, Tom had to make a choice, did he go down a failure spiral because he'd missed his goal, or did he choose to make the best of those he had in the room?

Tom chose to be pleased that he had 14 doctors in the room, to pride himself on his achievement and to draw on his self-efficacy to ensure that he ran a good seminar. At the end of the evening he had two new clients. This was fewer than he had hoped for, but he was 50% closer to his target than before he had set the goal. So Tom was pleased with his efforts, and rightly so.

Big, outrageous goals that match your dream and are congruent with your values do work. In being outrageous you have to treat the goal as a focus, direction and fun. If you make it – great; if you don't quite achieve the goal, you'll still be a lot closer to your dream than you would have been without it.

Box 4.2: Setting big goals

When you are setting big goals, make sure you:

1. Have absolute clarity about what you want.
2. Know what is at stake and what you are prepared to do.
3. Go all out for success and don't carry doubt with you.
4. Tie your goal in with your passion.
5. Approach the goal with an attitude of fun and value the experiences of the journey, whatever the outcome.

It takes courage and daring to put your dreams and goals out there, but when you do, great things happen.

CHAPTER 5

Step 4: Create a plan and take action

This really is quite straightforward. If you make a proper plan out of your dreams and goals, you are much more likely to succeed. Planning gives you the clarity and direction that you need to take targeted action. Taking action that moves you towards your dream is the true indicator of a Success Mindset.

There are three stages to this:

1. **Planning:** what you need to do, how and when.
2. **Obstacles:** the things (real and imaginary) that get in the way of your plan.
3. **Action:** actually doing stuff to realise your dream.

Planning

There is no one right way to plan. The way you record your plan, structure your plan and follow your plan is largely down to your personality, your working practices and your values. Not having a plan, however, will sabotage your business sooner or later. Your plan is not there to water down your dream, to rationalise it and to constrain you, it is there to help you keep moving in the right direction and to help you identify what action needs to be taken, when.

> Think of Dr Martin Luther King Jr. When he made his world-changing speech in 1963, and he talked about 'a dream' he had, many thought him unrealistic – many even thought his dream undesirable. He knew this would be the response, so what was he doing? He knew that if his dream was to be realised he needed a big plan. He

would face many obstacles and much opposition, so he would need to get through these to make his dream happen. When he made that speech he created a picture in people's minds, one that some had never thought of. He seeded the vision of a better reality. He took action towards his dream by inspiring others to believe in it too. He had a plan.

The speech was followed by more rallies, meetings and political lobbying. Step by step, he followed this plan, working towards his goal. His passion for his dream, his drive and his energy, captured the imagination of millions, and led them to action. Dr Martin Luther King Jr. and his team planned for this, they structured their activity to make it happen. Without a plan, his dream would not have been realised.

The trick with an effective plan is to keep it simple. It is the clarity and direction that gives you the power to achieve. Your plan in this context is different from a formal business plan. Your plan for success is a road map: you are at A and you want to get to B. When you look at the map there are many routes you can take that will get you to B. You choose the one that looks and feels right at the time. Along the way you may find there are diversions; there may also be short-cuts because you found a better way. Overall, the direction of travel stays the same and the destination is reached.

A clear picture that takes you towards your dream and enables you to achieve your goals massively increases your chances of success. To really work, this picture, or plan has to stay live and flexible. Its job is to create manageable steps, reduce the feeling of overwhelm and prevent you from getting pulled off course. It allows you to get real clarity of purpose, to become excited and to be compelled to act.

Box 5.1: Creating a plan

1. Follow your heart and your passion and stay true to your dream
2. Understand what you need in order to succeed at each stage:

   a. What do you need to know?
   b. Who do you need to involve or engage with?
   c. What resources do you need?
   d. What is your time-frame?

3. What are the key steps along the way?
4. What action do you need to take?

Obstacles

Obstacles fall into three categories: the material ones, those that occur along your journey and the self-induced ones.

The material obstacles are the ones that make pursuing your dream practically difficult. They include things like financial and family commitments; your health or fitness; your current skill and knowledge base; and your contacts, connections and profile in your industry. None of these are insurmountable if you work them into your plan. If you truly believe that is impossible, your obstacle belongs in the third category.

The second category of obstacles occurs because of events or circumstances that you encounter on your journey. The key to overcoming them is how you react; your behaviour, your attitude and, most of all, the action you take. Everyone perceives circumstances differently; it is how you perceive a situation that makes the difference. How you respond impacts on those around you; the passion and energy that you share will impact hugely on how others react to circumstances. Choose to interpret obstacles and events in a way that empowers and reinforces your path to success. This may mean looking at your map again and finding a different route; it may mean going back a little and learning what you need to learn from the journey; and it may also mean just holding on, maintaining your focus and riding the bumps. If you can't find a way to learn and progress, you should check that your obstacle does not belong in the third group, the self-induced ones (Box 5.2).

Self-induced obstacles stem from a perceived lack, from fear and from attitude. They can stop you from taking action altogether. They are the most dangerous category of obstacles because they are internal and – in some part of your unconscious – they are there to protect you. The good news is that by developing your Success Mindset you will identify and tackle these obstacles.

Box 5.2: The key self-induced obstacles

Fear	Knowledge
Laziness	Despair
Complacency	Overwhelm

Fear

Fear is an innate emotion designed to protect us. It reminds us to pay attention, notice what is happening to us and, critically, do something about it. This is why the emotion of fear triggers the flight or fight response our forefathers needed to get out of danger. The problem is that not much of the fear we face today is real, mortal danger, or any other kind of physical danger. Most of the fear we face now is a psychological fear, often internally constructed. People create fears based on their values, their beliefs about themselves, their experiences, and to keep themselves safe and free from risk. Big fears related to setting up a business include fear of failure, of success, of ridicule, of lack of money, of not being good enough, etc.

Some of this fear is conjured up because we overthink stuff and imagine so many variants, different scenarios and what-if's that we finish up confused and paralysed. A huge amount of energy and time is consumed by fear, but it gets you nowhere; rather like a rocking chair really.

The only real way out of fear is to take action and move through the fear. Before you can do this you need to understand what, specifically, you are afraid of, where it comes from and what you are prepared to do to resolve it. If you are not prepared to take action in the direction of your dream because of fear (or 'good reasons', as you probably call them), then you need to go back to Step 1, work with your values and identify what is holding you back.

Case study 5: Facing the fear

Frances had always wanted to be a coach, to do something more meaningful, as she saw it, but she struggled with her fear, and it stopped her from committing fully to what she really wanted to do. Frances was made redundant from her job as an HR assistant and decided to retrain as a coach. She spent much of her redundancy package on retraining, did all of her practical coaching time and became qualified. By the time I met Frances she was working as a secretary because, she said, she'd 'run out of money'. She had wanted to train to use 360° feedback because she thought it would help her get some coaching clients. It didn't.

The problem wasn't with Frances's coaching skills; it was because she couldn't put her effort and energy into her new coaching business. She believed that she wouldn't get clients and feared not having enough money to meet her commitments. This stopped Frances from really engaging with her potential clients, not least because she already had a full-time job. She didn't operate with power or passion and lacked conviction in her own ability to succeed, and this showed big time. Frances recognised her position and her self-sabotage, but lacked the desire to do anything about it.

Then the crunch came. Frances was offered a promotion in her secretarial role; she took it, saying that she could always return to coaching later. One of two things happened here. Either, having a coaching business was not really Frances's true passion, so that when the time came to make some risky choices she didn't want the business enough. Alternatively, Francis did want to have her own coaching business but she couldn't move beyond her fear to really commit to it; neither did she value herself enough to get some help or coaching – despite having a network of peers from her coaching training who volunteered to help her.

The thing about fear is that until you face it, it will keep coming back, presenting slightly different situations but in the same cycle. In the end you have to take some action, either to move through your fear or to avoid it.

Laziness

In the end, setting up and maintaining a business, whether it's built on your dream and passion or not, takes time, effort and work. If it is easier to just sit and watch television it could be that you are procrastinating through fear, self-doubt or overwhelm. It might also mean that you are not prepared to put the required effort into this particular dream. Be honest with yourself and deal with what you find kindly.

Complacency

Most people need to feel motivated either towards or away from a specific outcome before they take action. If the gain or the pain is not great enough to motivate you may well get stuck, your plan done but no action being taken. If this is the case, revisit your dream and your goals: are they big enough to compel you to action? If your business is just cruising along, it's good enough and you're good enough, then why would you need to do more? Many people seem content to live a mediocre life. If that's you and you really are content, then that's OK. If you're not content, you feel miserable or that something is missing but you lack the motivation to do anything about it, then it is not OK. Just check that you are not settling for less than you really want out of life – and if you are, consider why.

Knowledge

If you don't have the skills, education or experience required for the next step of your plan, this can stop you from acting. Not knowing how to do something, or what the next step is, can derail your big dream. Acknowledge that you can't know everything on your journey and do something about it. Find someone who does know to help you, go and learn, or even adjust your route; do something to keep you moving.

Despair

You have tried everything in your business or life and it doesn't work for you. Even when someone else tries to help with a solution, you know it won't work because you've tried it before. Ask yourself what boundary conditions are running your life, and then deal with them.

Overwhelm

This happens when you don't have a clear plan, you try to do too many things at once, or you overthink things. If you are feeling overwhelmed, make sure that your plan is clear and get back in touch with why your big dream is important to you. Then break your goals into smaller chunks and tackle those that are easy or quick wins first. This reduces stress and starts to get you into a Success Mindset. The very fact that you are doing something reduces your capacity for overthinking the stuff you're not doing yet.

Action

If you don't already know it (and I'm sure you do), the key to success is to take action. The way to achieve your dream is to make it happen. Action for its own sake is not enough. Planned, targeted action in pursuit of your plan is what is needed.

Action conquers fear. For me, it's a bit like a rollercoaster ride. I don't like them much, but until a couple of years ago my son was too young to ride without an adult. Waiting in the queue, I feel the anxiety rise; as we get in the car, all I can think is 'It will be over soon'; and as we climb slowly to the first big dip, I feel sick to the pit of my stomach. Then WHAM!! The car descends at speed, a few twirls and spins, and it's all over. What's left is a feeling of exhilaration, excitement and a satisfaction that I've done it. And later, when we recount the stories of our day, it's the thrill and excitement of the ride that's remembered, not the dread beforehand.

The principle is the same, whatever the fear. Your first sales pitch, public speaking, writing a report, taking an exam, anywhere that your performance comes under scrutiny; even more so when it's your own self-imposed scrutiny. Take some action and blast away your fear – or at the very least, start to reduce it.

Overthinking an issue is exactly the same, and taking some action will break the cycle. You can't think yourself into a new way of acting, but you can act in a way that develops a new pattern of thinking.

Box 5.3: Staying on the road to success

The trick to taking action that keeps you on your route to success is:

- Keep your plan simple, so it's easy to know what action to take
- Start small and do the stuff that builds confidence and comfort
- Keep stretching that comfort zone
- Check you progress regularly
- Don't to be afraid to take a detour or short-cut when one is needed
- Stay focused on living the dream

CHAPTER 6

Step 5: Apply personal excellence to everything

To apply personal excellence is to excel in whatever you do. To excel actually means to have improved, done better than before, or surpassed expectation. Personal excellence is a mindset activity. It is a way of conditioning yourself to achieve. It's also a way of operating in the world. Personal excellence doesn't just happen overnight; it takes practice and training to ensure that your best self is the one that engages with life.

Applying personal excellence takes self-belief and commitment; it also requires you to be present in whatever you are doing, not thinking about what's next or what's for tea. Operating in the now, being consumed by what you are doing and giving it your full attention is the best way to achieve a state of personal excellence. You can choose to practise excellence at any time – you don't have to have all your ducks in a row before you start.

Box 6.1: Developing a style of excellence

Developing excellence requires:

- Discipline
- Emotional control
- Attitude
- Courage
- Calmness

Discipline

Discipline is about pushing yourself beyond your comfort zone, facing the things you find difficult and consistently working towards your dream. For the most part, if you are following your dream, many of your activities will be fun and come from your heart, the very act of doing them inspires you and energises you. It's easy to apply personal excellence to all you do. Often, the activities that take you forward can also make you feel vulnerable, take you into stretch zones and call into question your direction and commitment. This is where the discipline comes in: remain focused on your specific goal while keeping in touch with the bigger dream, remember the purpose behind your activity and trust yourself to move forward.

It's unrealistic to assume that everything you do in life will fill you with passion and excitement. As with all things that are worth having, there will be some activities that are more routine and less in tune with your natural talents. You may need to apply some discipline to actually get these done. Life, and certainly running your own business, has its fair share of drudgery jobs, the ones that you just have to get done and out of the way. If you're practising personal excellence, apply it to these jobs too. Giving them your full attention, focusing on the benefit of completing the job, rather than on the work itself, will make doing them a more pleasant experience. It will also mean that you do a better job.

If you approach the task with a sense of boredom and begrudge the job, it's unlikely you will gain any satisfaction from it. The job will be unlikely to get your full attention, and as a result may not be done well. While this may not appear to matter for some tasks, if this is your default approach to jobs you don't like, the attitude becomes a habit and can result in reduced fulfilment and enjoyment across a range of activities. This in turn brings poorer results and creates a destructive cycle. By committing to excellence in everything you do, this will become your default response or habit, making personal excellence where it really matters that much easier to achieve. Apply some discipline to the way you work, commit fully to whatever you do, be present in the task, focus on the benefits and give it your best efforts. Then just see what happens to your results.

Emotional control

This is about self-awareness, knowing what takes you off track, what triggers self-doubt and other unhelpful emotions that keep you from working with excellence. Much of this emotional control comes down to state management – your state being your present condition, the behaviour and subjective expression you display and the prism through which you see the world at any given time. This is governed by your neurology (including emotions), physiology and biochemistry. Personal excellence is one of many states that filter your interpretation of what you are experiencing. There are also very many unhelpful states that prevent you from achieving, focusing and working with ease and commitment. Maintaining personal excellence therefore necessitates a few strategies to create state changes. If you've studied NLP you will likely already be aware of these. If you haven't, here are a few simple strategies to break negative or unhelpful states and regain excellence. Your mental and physiological processes are interconnected – you can't change one without affecting the other. This means that a simple change in your physiological state can create a change in your emotional state.

A common example that most of us will have experienced is deep breathing to induce relaxation. Several things are happening here that change both our physiological and our neurological state. Physiologically, the slowing of breathing inhibits sympathetic nerve activity and increases parasympathetic nerve activity. Very simply, this reduces the output of hormones such as adrenaline and cortisol that stimulate activity, like the flight or fight response. This in turn regulates and improves cardiovascular function and digestive function and reduces muscle tension, returning the body to its rest state. Neurologically, two key factors influence how we feel: first, deep breathing has a similar effect to laughing and exercise in that it induces the release of endorphins, creating a natural mood lift. Second, because we are consciously focusing on breathing, other, unwanted stuff such as self-talk is pushed away. Together these create a change in your physical and mental state which in effect changes your emotional state. It is useful to be able to create a state change for yourself when unhelpful states such as anxiety creep in, or when you are feeling stressed or fearful about something. It is often these negative states around what you are trying to achieve or how you are progressing towards your goal that throw you off track.

Another example is the effect of a stimulus, such as your favourite empowering music. The physical act of hearing something familiar creates a neurological association with power, passion, energy, or whatever that music means to you, and your emotional state is changed. Getting up and moving around if you've been sitting at your desk for a while has the same effect. The challenge is to have a few state breaks that you know empower you; because these will allow you to move yourself back to a state of personal excellence more easily. Some further examples of state management techniques can be found in the bibliography at the end of the book.

Attitude

Maintaining an attitude of excellence is easier when you stick to your values. When your goal is something you really believe in it is much easier to shine, to feel motivated and therefore to get inspired enough to strive for excellence. Most people in their zone of excellence have a can-do attitude; they take risks that move them toward their goal and they are happy to share their passion for their subject. This is contagious, and it motivates and captures others as well as you. When you operate from a state of personal excellence, attitudes towards disappointment and negative outcomes are also different. It is much easier to treat these experiences as something to be learned from rather than as major setbacks. Given that attitude is a choice, excellence simply needs a bit of practice.

Courage

Courage is about acting from your heart and not letting fear dominate your life; it is not about an absence of fear. As discussed above, fear is both necessary and useful in driving us toward our dreams. Courage is about knowing when to face fears and take some action. It is also about having enough inner belief or self-efficacy to take action, even when there is a risk that the outcome might damage your perception of yourself, or leave you exposed to criticism or ridicule by others. Courage is also about conquering any boundary conditions and inner beliefs that are sabotaging or could sabotage your success. You cannot operate from a state of personal excellence without being courageous.

Courage is also about not settling for less than you want or less than the dream that you are passionate about. We all know people who've settled for less, and maybe we have done it ourselves at times. There's no place for settling for less when practising personal excellence; the two are a total contradiction. Settling for less is a self-protection mechanism. Not having what you want or not achieving a goal is uncomfortable, even unpleasant, and so you set up a self-protection strategy. Rationalising why something couldn't work for you, justifying why it didn't quite happen this time, even blaming others, serves to lessen the pain. Instead of looking calmly at what can be done differently and how your dream can be achieved, what you have is made to look attractive. Defeat sets in because it has all become too hard. The really sad thing about this is that the defeat often sets in before any real effort has been expended and before any action has been taken.

Case study 6: Finding courage

I have known James, a potential client, for some time now. He has his own marketing business, mostly providing internet services to one particular client. I have met him at a number of networking events; he's always there with his cards, his leaflets and a good story about what his business will do. James has been on my mailing list for a couple of years; he attends many of my free business development events, and those of my industry colleagues, but he has never committed to any real action or serious investment to develop his business in line with the dream he talks about. At a recent workshop James had the opportunity to take part in a business focus session on stage. The object of the session was to identify where we are sabotaging our own businesses.

As James described his dream, which was to provide niche marketing and coaching to accountants, he interspersed his passion with reasons why he couldn't do it. Many of his reasons were financial; he couldn't afford to get trained in business development, he couldn't afford to exhibit at shows and advertise like his successful competitors did, and he didn't have any money to employ a secretary to help him. A few questions about why James had chosen to coach accountants revealed that he had trained and worked as an accountant in his early career, but he felt frustrated by the lack of vision and went off to learn about marketing instead. The client James currently worked with was in manufacturing, and James was really doing an interim marketing role not consulting. He talked with great passion and excitement about what he could do for accountants but didn't have the courage to really apply himself to doing it. Instead, he had created a load of really strong beliefs about why he couldn't pursue his passion.

The key question here is how valid are James's beliefs and do they serve him? James had not actually approached any accountants with his offering, other than those he'd come across at networking meetings. Neither had he used his marketing skills to create something specific for accountants – he was too busy with the one client he did have. In fact, he'd put a lot of thought into his dream business, but very little effort and no action. Somewhere along the way James had decided that it was too hard and he had created a way out. He had a client who paid him as much as he needed, he didn't want to risk losing that, and he probably couldn't compete with others in the field because he lacked financial resources. The result? He had paralysed himself through lack of courage and his self-limiting behaviour, and then settled for what he already had.

Except that's not what really happens. James's still keeps showing up, he still talks with some passion about his dream, and when the opportunity for a free on-stage session presented itself, he was up and out of his chair in a flash. He may have settled for less, but his dream is still there, nagging at him, making him envy those who have what he wants. James can't achieve his dream because he has focused his effort and energy on what is missing, what he cannot do and what he doesn't have. This doesn't make for a happy and fulfilled life.

If you're wondering about the outcome of the on-stage session, I asked James what he did know and what he could offer to accountants by way of marketing that wouldn't cost him the money he didn't have, something his competitors might not be doing. After some digging around we came up with a 'marketing tips' report that he could use by way of an introduction to local accountants, requesting an opportunity to meet them after they had read it. James committed to doing this. I have to admit that I was a little unconvinced. I suggested that he could send the report to me first to look at – thus creating further accountability for him. I received a copy of James's report recently and it was a good piece of work, offering real value to potential clients. I hope he finds the courage to pursue his dream – because there is a business there, for sure.

The thing about settling for less is that when what we want looks too far away, we convince ourselves that it's not possible, filing our dreams away in our subconscious. Those dreams stay there, they don't go away; every now and then they pop up to haunt us. Pay attention to these haunting whispers: they are important, they are our path to personal excellence.

Calmness

Very simply, calmness is about grace in the face of adversity. If something doesn't go to plan, review and learn what needs to be learned from the adversity and then re-plan from a position of calm, not reaction. Calmness is also being able to manage people - your clients, colleagues and even loved ones, when they don't support your excellence. Usually this is about creating strategies to protect yourself from their energy, not banishing them from your life. Maintaining focus on your goal or dream helps you to remain calm.

Practising excellence

Excellence only comes with practice. Striving for personal excellence also requires practice and some resilience. A good starting-point is to look after yourself, to nourish your body and mind. This includes the obvious things like eating healthily, exercising and getting enough sleep. It also includes what you expose yourself to by way of mental stimulus – so do things that re-fill your well. We all need some down time: what you read, what you watch on TV and whom you talk to all impact on your sense of personal excellence, so choose how you spend your time well.

Box 6.2: Practising excellence

1. Focus on one thing at a time and master it.
2. Don't have failures, have experiences. Learn from them and move on, don't dwell on them.
3. Excellence is easier to achieve when those around you know what you're about, what you're aiming for, so share your dream, ideas and vision with those who matter to you and those who can help you.
4. When sharing and selling your dream, focus on what you can do for others, the power and benefits to people.
5. Accept that perfection does not exist. When you know that you have done your best move on.
6. Most of all, in the quest for excellence, do only what you can be proud of.

If you are prepared to work at it, you can apply personal excellence in whatever you put your passion, energy and focus into. To really go for excellence, you need to be the best version of yourself that you can be – and not try to be someone else's idea of excellence or to live their passion.

CHAPTER 7

Step 6: Maintain persistent focus

Maintaining focus is perhaps one of the hardest parts of following your dream. It is also one of the absolutely critical factors in success. Many things influence where your focus lies, and concentrating your effort and energy in the long term requires active intervention, not just a dream and a few goals, because when the going gets tough your focus will drift, and so will your energy and your chances of success. Many good businesses have been sabotaged by lack of focus.

Like the other aspects of the Success Mindset, focus is about retraining and practice. I say retraining because, as small children, we all knew how to focus. Something would capture our imagination, like a particular toy, often the one that another child was playing with, and we maintained focus on it until we either got it or were actively distracted by something better. We've not lost that ability to focus, we just have more distractions. Part of the Success Mindset is being able to train ourselves to focus on what we want. Once we know what the dream or the goals are along the way, focus is about the ability to persist, or to try different methods if the original plan goes off course or doesn't deliver the required results.

Thomas Edison is a good example of this. His dream was to give light to every home; he focused on his dream and eventually he achieved it. He experienced many challenges and unsuccessful attempts along the way, but his persistent focus enabled him to create a system – including the incandescent light bulb – that provided homes with light. In fact he was not the first to develop the light bulb; there were more than 20 others before him. His

light bulb was better, and it was his system for supplying
electricity to homes that made the light in every home
a reality. Edison's personal resolve, focus and ability to
overcome obstacles enabled him to realise his dream.

You get what you focus your attention on, so it's worth focusing on
success and not difficulty, your opportunities and not obstacles. This
is where you also need to check your habitual focus, as focusing on
the wrong things can sabotage your success. What we pay attention
to forms deep neurological activity, or our default reactions, which
can empower or hinder us. It's worth paying attention to where your
attention goes by default, and then identifying and reprogramming
unhelpful patterns.

Maintaining focus is also about maintaining the energy and passion
in your dream. A good example of this is the buzz you get from
attending a motivational seminar. We've all been to them; they are
about subjects not dissimilar to this section of the book: how you
become empowered, the importance of goals. The thing they do
most is raise the energy levels in the room to the extent that we
do things we may not do in other environments. We do things like
shout out our goals to hundreds of strangers, we rush round hugging
and high-fiving people we don't know, and we frantically write
down outrageous goals that in that moment, in that room, we are
absolutely committed to achieving. Those goals probably do reflect
some of our innermost dreams, and the level of energy generated
in that room at that moment allowed us to reach right in and get
them out – in itself a useful exercise. But what happens when we
come away from the seminar? Despite a handful of business cards,
a real sense of excitement and having had a fab time, many of us
will put the book with the goals written in it away in the drawer, and
a few days later, the energy from the room gone, will get back to
normal. Apart from having had a glimpse of our potential we will
remain largely untouched by our experience. This is not the same
for everyone, of course. Some people will keep a few contacts,
revisit and work on their goals from the event and help to shape their
development. For a lucky few, real shift does happen. Something
touched them at a deep neurological level that changed their focus

and created some real drive, persistence and energy, enabling them to really connect with and focus on their dream.

I'm not knocking this type of event – in fact I'm a frequent attender myself. What I am saying is that the thing that makes you successful once you've identified your dream is focus and energy in the direction you need to go. So here are a few tips for staying focused despite the day-to-day distractions and pressures for your attention.

Box 7.1: Maintaining focus

1. Have well-defined goals.
2. Break it down into actionable chunks.
3. Prioritise.
4. Focus on what you can control.
5. Track your progress.
6. Reward yourself.
7. Make time to work on your dream persistently.
8. Accept that it will be hard at times.

Have well-defined goals

Be clear about your goals and be sure that they are what you really want (see Step 3).

Break it down into actionable chunks

Ensure that you have a plan to get from where you are to your dream, in detailed chunks; then focus on what is achievable in the short term as well as on the big dream (see Step 4).

Prioritise

Focus on the things that need to happen to let you move to the next stage. Sometimes something will demand your urgent attention. Dealing with important issues quickly will also help you to retain focus. Procrastinating and putting off the things that you are challenged by or not so interested in will dilute your focus and drain your energy, so take action.

Focus on what you can control

Base your success on things you can influence or control, not on external factors. Not only can you not control what other people think or do, you can also waste a lot of energy and time worrying about what you can't control.

Track your progress

It's easy at the start to focus on your dream and to see how you are moving forward, but as tasks get harder and distractions become stronger retaining commitment can be difficult. This is where careful tracking of what has been achieved, what works well and what can be done differently helps to maintain focus. It's easy to see what still needs to be achieved, but you can also see how far you have come.

Reward yourself

Rewarding yourself for what you've achieved helps to maintain motivation and encourages you to focus on what is left to do.

Make time to work on your dream persistently

It's important to work towards your goal or dream regularly and persistently. Setting aside specific time often works best. It's often good to pick your most creative time. This doesn't have to be too regimented; if you work better in the mornings, for example, set aside a little time each morning to keep in touch with your dream, and longer chunks to actually move towards it. Personally, I work better at night, and most of this book, my previous one and most of my college assignments have been written in the small hours.

Accept that it will be hard at times

You are in this for the long haul, it will be difficult at times, so make sure that you have support and that those close to you know and understand your goal. Ask for help from those who have been there before and those you whom trust and respect. Most of all, be kind to yourself.

CHAPTER 8
Step 7: Invest in yourself

One of the biggest business sabotages is ignorance. Not knowing what is going on in your business, not knowing how to market your business, not knowing enough about your industry or not understanding finances. All of these undermine your ability to perform well, but even worse, they can destroy your confidence and stop you from moving forward with your business. A powerful mindset is an educated one. I'm not specifically talking about academic qualifications here; this is about the personal, social, practical and financial behaviours that make a difference to how you interact, perform and achieve.

"Education is freedom, it's the only way out."

Oprah Winfrey

Someone with a Success Mindset is constantly seeking new information, challenging their thinking and perceptions and evolving their goals and plan if necessary. Knowledge gives you freedom, choice and power. Success comes from consistently expanding your knowledge base. Many coaches I know have limiting beliefs about their business knowledge: this holds them back and makes them vulnerable. Knowledge is a bit like fear, really: you need to take action to resolve the situation. There is a deluge of information available to people wanting to set up, run and grow their own people development business. Much of it is available free on the internet, so there really is no excuse for being ill informed. Yet many in our industry are. I guess that if you are reading this book you are interested in growing your business, you are prepared to take action to learn what you need to know and you are prepared to invest your time in your own development. All of these are prerequisites for a Success Mindset.

Case study 7: Investing in yourself

Patricia has a consultancy business of some years' standing. She started to use 360° feedback with her health sector clients to support some organisational development work she was doing. She got on well with the hospital and they quite rightly respected her as an experienced consultant.

When we set up the 360° feedback project Patricia said that she was happy with it; she knew how to use the system and understood about feedback facilitation, as she'd been doing consultancy for years. Some weeks into the project she phoned me to say that she was unhappy because the reports needed someone to do face-to-face feedback with the client. She felt that she would be out of pocket after purchasing the 360° feedback and then delivering to the client.

What Patricia had missed in her hurry to tell me that she knew all about how to use 360° feedback was the value of her time, and how our 360° feedback coaches make their money. In treating the 360° feedback like a psychometric tool she had under-quoted to her client. After some discussion I realised that there were two aspects to Patricia's situation. First, she didn't want to admit that this was the first time she'd used 360° feedback and therefore hadn't asked for (or been offered) the support she needed – most of which would have been free through our practitioner network. Second, not wanting to appear ignorant, out of date or weak had made her commercially vulnerable. As it happened, Patricia had some capacity to integrate the feedback sessions into time when she was already on site at the hospital, so it didn't cost her in real terms.

Patricia has since been on our practitioner training course and regularly uses 360° feedback with her clients. Armed with her new knowledge, she now weaves in individual feedback sessions, organisational learning recommendations and facilitated group follow-up. Patricia says it was lucky that she got into 360° feedback because it's generating follow-up business with her existing clients. Of course, it's not luck at all. Because she educated herself, she now sees opportunities that she couldn't see before – and she acts on them.

Investing in yourself is about having the confidence to spend on your development where it is indicated. When you do spend on your development make sure that it's on what you need to learn, not what you want to learn. We naturally migrate toward things and people we're interested in, so be mindful that any investment you make in yourself moves you closer to your dream.

It's not just the things you read and watch, or the courses you go on that impact on your success. The counsel you keep, the role models you choose and the behaviour you emulate all have an impact. Many people seek advice, mentorship even, from people they know in business – for example their own family members or more experienced friends. These people may or may not be successful or share the same sorts of dreams or aspirations. Although their advice is given with love and support, too often the bar is set too low, potential is sabotaged and we replicate their patterns instead of following our own dreams.

Choosing business mentors and role models is a very personal thing. You need to find people whose values and actions you are comfortable with, and who at the same time stretch and challenge your own thinking and position. What is critical is that you choose people who are achieving success themselves. Good mentors bridge the gap between where you are and where you want to be.

If you can't access top-class mentors at this stage, learn by reading about successful people, study what it is that they do, and then model their behaviour.

Exercise 3: Role modelling

Model one of your favourite business gurus.

- What is the psychology behind their success?
- Identify their

    - attributes
    - attitude
    - values
    - drivers
    - beliefs about themselves
    - skills and strategy
    - decision-making processes.

- How do they communicate?
- What inspires them?

When you have identified some of the factors that make your role model successful, implement them in your own life, and monitor any changes.

Your peer group is also important; who you spend time with impacts on how you invest in yourself. If you are already the most successful one in the group you are less likely to be striving for further excellence. If you hang out with people who are better off, more successful and who inspire you, you are more likely to expand your knowledge and increase your business success.

Investing in yourself is about raising your game, creating opportunities to play a bigger game and giving yourself the confidence and skill to get out there and take action towards your dream.

Seven Steps to a Success Mindset

If you read and adopt the Seven Steps to a Success Mindset you can transform both your outlook on your business and your ability to make your dream a reality.

A powerful Success Mindset is your best attribute ever. It will enable you to get the best out of a situation, to increase your presence, passion and energy. Most of all, it will give you choices: the choice to follow your dream, the ability to overcome obstacles and the choice to take the action you need to take to make your dream a reality.

Ultimately everyone has the same ability to control their mind and move beyond internal and external barriers to success. The way you choose to do this, the attitude you take, determines whether you succeed or whether you sabotage your business.

PART 2
Your business

This part of the book is about your business, its growth and development. The things you will learn here apply to your whole business, whether or not you use 360° feedback as part of your model. This is the skill set part of your journey; the book will show you how to get noticed, how to clarify your offering and how to start building profitable relationships with your potential clients. In the first instance, applying these principles will help you to determine your business priorities, get organised and develop the business goals that will help you to achieve your dream.

The principles and strategies discussed are from the 360 Profit Programme. They are strategies that I, and many other successful business owners, use as a matter of course in our own businesses. The recipe works it is a question of acquiring the right skill set, deciding on the priorities for your own business and then taking action. This part of the book will help you to focus on what you need to do and in what order.

Chapters 14 and 15, consider how the addition of a well-known tool or product, in this case 360° feedback, can strengthen your business model, attract new clients and enable you offer more to your existing clients.

CHAPTER 9

Know what you want

Just in case you skipped Part 1 (after all, you do that stuff for a living), here's a quick reminder. For your business to grow and succeed you need a plan – some goals driven by what you are passionate about and can really get behind when the hard work sets in. So make sure that you know what, specifically, you are trying to achieve, and that you have your end in mind. Businesses that float along, taking work as it crops up, whatever that work is, are both less satisfying and less profitable for the business owner. Be bold, be ostentatious – and carve out the business of your dreams.

To do this you need to spend time on the strategy stuff, understanding where you are going, as well as identifying what you want to do and with whom. The next step is to decide how close your existing business is to your dream. Knowing how close or far from your dream you are will help you to identify the action needed to get to where you want to be. This part of the book will help you to identify the areas you need to think about, and to prioritise your actions. It doesn't matter how much you plan, how much you know or how big your dreams are; if you don't take focused action towards what you want, you are sabotaging your business.

Measure everything

Action is the key to business success, and that action needs to be targeted and persistent to deliver results. The people development industry is full of coaches and consultants talking about taking action and using measurable or SMART goals, but only a small percentage of them genuinely apply this principle to their own business. The fundamental way of knowing whether a strategy is working or an action is moving you closer to your goal is to measure its outcome.

At a very basic level this applies to your business finances. Understand exactly what is happening. What does your bank account tell you? What does your cash flow look like on a monthly and annual basis, and how does this measure up to your projections? A poll of coaches at a conference I went to recently revealed that about half of them didn't know their monthly cash flow, and a third didn't know how much was in their bank account (within a few pounds). This is a basic, easy measure that tells you if your business is on the right track, on target for your dream, or if you need to take different action. It is the very minimum that every small business owner should know.

Furthermore, to start to get really serious about growing your business, you need to know all of your costs relating to client acquisition. You need to know what your real costs are for each of the products and services you offer, and therefore what your margins are. This way you can identify where your real profit is coming from and focus on the activities that create the biggest benefit – and refrain from taking action for the sake of it.

It isn't just money that needs to be measured, though. Marketing activity needs to be treated with exactly the same degree of rigour. Look closely at where you put your marketing effort, what it is costing you and what specific return you're getting. Do this by tracking where clients come from, whether they are people you've met at events or who have responded to some form of offer, information or advertising. This will be discussed in more detail in Chapter 10 when we look at marketing, but the bottom line is that if some specific action has the potential to influence your business growth, measure it. If it works, do more of it; and if it doesn't, don't keep doing it.

Assume nothing

Think about how well you really know your clients. Do you understand their real wants and what it is that they are actually buying – because you can be fairly sure that it is not your product. They will be buying an outcome of some sort – a benefit or a solution, something that makes their lives easier. It is essential that you understand what your clients want, because then you can ensure that your marketing activity is directed towards demonstrating the outcomes they are looking for.

Case study 8: Knowing your clients

When Appraisal360 changed its Customer Relationship Management (CRM) system in 2011 we used the change over to ensure that we really knew what our clients wanted. We asked our existing clients to give us feedback and information to help us to offer the right 360 products and services to the right people. We had two different versions of the questionnaire; one for our corporate clients and one for the coaches and consultants who use the system with their own clients or deliver parts of the service package for our corporate clients through our 360 practitioner network.

We made the process quick and easy for people to complete, using tick boxes and multiple-choice questions and providing an opportunity for them to give free text answers. This also made the data easier to analyse and act on. We asked people on our mailing list a number of questions we already held information about, like their demographic profile, their industry sector and company size, the types of products or services our clients had bought and what they'd been most pleased with. The reason we did this was to check that we were describing things in the same way as our clients; to check that our client information was still accurate; and to ensure that we understand what they liked about our service. We also asked what else they might be interested in, from a range of offerings. Their answers frequently reflected products or services we already offered; these products that were packaged or presented differently and the client didn't recognised them. Finally, we asked if there were things that we didn't offer that they would find useful; and what they believed their main challenges were. For the corporates, these were appraisal, giving feedback and getting the most out of their teams. For the coaches and development consultants, the issues were focused more on business growth, getting clients, making money out of 360° feedback, and the really big one – being able to sell it.

This information has enabled us to significantly improve our customer service, offer the right things to the right clients and be really targeted in ensuring that our products and services satisfy our clients' most wanted outcomes. The 360 Profit Programme is a direct result of this work. The information we got from clients enabled us to take our existing business development programme and stuff it full of practical help; and to create opportunities for participants to really get to work on their own business. For those who choose to use 360° feedback as part of their model, we have to created more of a 'business in a box' approach to the way the programme runs. These changes have made the programme even more beneficial for coaches and consultants, and more fun to work with too.

As a result of this exercise we now have the evidence to support our belief that we have three discrete client groups. We also have three independent marketing strategies and we have improved our responsiveness to each group.

When did you last ask your customers what they wanted, why they did business with you and what else they might like? To some extent, the size of your business and the number of clients you want to profile will influence the way you gather information; a telephone survey, a postal questionnaire or an email questionnaire all have merit. The key to getting the information returned is to ask people for their help. Then make it easy for them, ensure that it's not too time consuming and explain why you are asking for the information. Calling your survey market research or updating information are both great ways to sabotage your response rate.

Be distinctive

Differentiate your business. This is the best way to stand out in a crowded market. Make sure that you know what others in your particular area of people development are doing, and know where the differences are. These often reflect the values and drivers behind your business – things like quality, trust, service standards, integrity, people focus, availability and price. If you are struggling to differentiate your business, revisit some of the values you identified in Part 1.

These differentiators will help you to develop your USP (unique selling proposition). Many coaches I've worked with say they are generalists and don't have a USP; however, not one of them has failed to find their USP or UVP (unique value proposition) with a bit of effort and a structured approach. Your full USP – or, if you like, the story of your business – needs to deal with the frustrations and fears that your potential clients have; it should talk about the outcomes they are looking for; and it must eliminate risk for potential clients. It provides a positioning statement about your business that sets you apart from your competitors.

Box 9.1: Defining your USP

1. Attract attention to your business.
2. Differentiate yourself.
3. Fill a perceived gap in the market.
4. Inspire or motivate people to take action.
5. Answer the 'Why should I buy from you?' question.

Being clear about what your business stands for will allow you to develop shorter versions that tie in to your brand identity and enable you to communicate your message with confidence. However, you are still looking to meet the criteria of a good USP. (Box 9.1)

A good USP cuts through the clutter – or, if you like, the noise – about all that your business does. A good USP gives you the clarity to present your offer using the key action triggers, or motivators for your potential client. It's not just a slogan or a statement that says you are the biggest, the best etc. It has to be something that has meaning to your clients and that differentiates you in their eyes, not yours (Box 9.2).

Box 9.2: Examples of great USPs

L'Oreal	'Because you're worth it'
Coca Cola	'It's the real thing'
Appraisal360	'online. fast. simple.'
Avis	'We try harder'

Get your USP right, and people should be asking you for more information, how you do what you claim to do, what your website address is and whether they can discuss things further with you.

Business growth

There are three primary ways to increase your business turnover:

1. Increase the number of clients you have.
2. Increase the average purchase value per client.
3. Increase the frequency of purchasing.

Often coaches focus any marketing effort that they make on number 1, which is actually the hardest of the three. To some extent you'll be starting from scratch: identifying a client, building up a new relationship and creating enough familiarity and trust for them to buy from you. Two and three – making a little more money from each client or increasing the frequency with which they buy from you – are generally easier. A little earlier in the book we mentioned measuring and knowing the margins on any sale, and this becomes critically important here. It's no good increasing turnover unless you are increasing profitability. Assuming that you know your numbers in terms of profit margin, Table 9.1 demonstrates what happens when you achieve a little more activity in each of the three business growth areas listed above.

Table 9.1: Increasing turnover and profitability

Number of Clients	Value of Client	Frequency of Purchase	Result
10	£200	2	£4,000
12	£200	2	£4,400
12	£250	2	£6,000
12	£250	3	£9,000

The example in Table 9.1 shows that getting two new clients increases turnover by 10%, but increasing the value of their spend has a bigger impact, and when you make small increases in all three areas of number, value and frequency the turnover more than doubles.

360° feedback clients

If you look at this model again, this time using the average pricing structure used by Appraisal360 feedback practitioners, the figures are even more striking because they represent something real (Table 9.2). Assume the practitioner has been asked to provide 360° feedback for 10 participants in a leadership programme. The value per individual client is £330 (online 360 and face-to-face feedback). The organisation wants to front-end its leadership programme, so they only need to purchase once per participant. The value of the contract is £3,300 (row 1). When the programme is set up a further two participants join, making the number of clients 12. This increases the contract value to £3,960 (row 2). Getting people to fill in questionnaires requires focus and effort and so, like many others, the organisation decides to outsource the administration to the 360 practitioner and add in some end-of-project management reports. This increases the cost per client to £350 and the contract value to £4,200. Finally, after some discussion about the purpose of the 360°

feedback the organisation concludes that it is a good idea to re-measure at the end of the leadership programme, and this raises the number of purchases from one to two. This doubles the value of the contract, to £8,400. The practitioner's investment will be slightly less than £1,000 in 360° feedback products and about 4 or 5 days' work. The proposition also offers a range of opportunities to identify further work from the outcomes of the 360 project.

Table 9.2: Turnover and profitability for 360 Practitioner

Number of Clients	Value of Client	Frequency of Purchase	Result
10	£330	1	£3,300
12	£330	1	£3,960
12	£350	1	£4,200
12	£350	2	£8,400

The thing about sustained business growth is to know your market, test what you are doing and repeat what works.

CHAPTER 10
Marketing plan

Marketing is a system for educating your potential clients, communicating the benefits of your product or service and accelerating their decision-making. Your job is to capture their hopes, desires and wants; and to identify with their fears, concerns and pain – and do something to create the solution or answer through your product or service. Your potential clients will buy an outcome that they can identify with, one that they value and one that provides a solution for whatever is driving them. Your job is to know your clients so well that you can build a marketing plan around the specific outcomes that they are looking for. Your marketing plan should include multiple approaches. Putting an advert in the local paper, meeting someone once at a networking event or sending an email newsletter or offer every now and then is unlikely to deliver much business.

Build relationships

Marketing is about building relationships – right from the off. A bad first impression is difficult to recover from, whether it be through online marketing activity, social media, an initial telephone conversation or face to face. The very first impression that you make on your clients determines their opinion of your business and, more importantly, whether they want to do business with you.

Case study 9: First impressions

When I think about the impact you have on people and the judgments people make about you, based on their initial impression, I always remember Sally a ward sister I used to coach in the NHS. Sally was a lovely lady, and very knowledgeable about her specialty, respiratory illnesses.

The nature of Sally's job meant that she frequently had to present her alternative model of care to members of the medical profession, hospital executives and various other non-clinical managers. Although her proposition was good for the patients in her care, Sally repeatedly failed to consider her proposal through the eyes of the other interested parties, the doctors and those with financial decision making power.

Sally would frequently arrive late for meetings, dressed in her, often dishevelled, nurse's uniform looking as if she had half of the hospital in her pockets. The impression Sally created was not that of the knowledgeable professional she was, but one of a passionate but misguided individual who didn't understand how things worked. It was easy for the doctors and executives to dismiss what Sally had to say because she didn't look like them, she didn't act like them and, most critically, she hadn't even attempted to sell her service in terms of its benefits to either group. The people Sally was trying to influence simply didn't buy into her story.

Basic as it sounds, Sally needed a change in her approach in order to sell what was actually a very good service. She needed to make a good first impression when she met with a group of doctors and managers – an impression of someone who they could trust, someone who was nearer their equal and who understood their concerns and anxieties about changing the way that patients were cared for.

While this may not feel like marketing, that's exactly what it was. Sally needed to offer something of value that solved a problem for those involved in the decision making about which services to fund. So we decided on a strategy. Sally went to the next meeting early, wearing a suit. By arriving early she got chance to talk to a couple of key people before the meeting. When she presented her vision for respiratory care it solved some of the capacity and cost issues faced by the hospital, reduced the pressure on doctors and provided a great service for patients. It was no real surprise when the team decided to pilot Sally's work.

The key to building relationships for marketing is no different from any other relationships we build. We need to establish rapport; we need the other person or people to trust us and, more than that, to really feel like we understand them, we speak their language and we can solve their problem. Once you start to develop a relationship with a potential client it needs to be sustained. It is no good having a conversation or an email exchange and then just leaving the trail to go cold. If you do, your potential clients may well have forgotten about you by the time they're ready to purchase; especially if your competitor has kept in touch. This is about staying visible, by direct contact, blog writing, speaking or being seen at key events, or any number of activities in your potential client's mind so that nothing can distract their attention and their business from you.

Educate your potential clients

This is your chance to tell your potential clients all about you, the products and services you offer and how these will help them. The challenge is to tell your potential clients enough about you, your company and your products to get them feeling that they know you and trust you. The key to success is to ensure that all the information you share adds value, in that it gives them something they didn't know before or it reframes something that is a problem for them. Everything should be presented in a way that reflects their values and that ensures your service is the right fit for them and, finally, it speaks directly to the emotional drivers that make their purchasing decision, the part of them that is looking for the right outcome. Most often this is their fear or pain. So your successful marketing material will confront this head on and, most importantly, offer a solution. To help you with this it's worth reading plenty of marketing copy and blogs from others within the personal development industry, to understand what they are doing and to get a feel for what effect their material has on you. Don't restrict yourself to looking at people development; there is a lot to be learned from other industries marketing technics too. When you get a picture of what is working and what you are comfortable with you can then model the effective practises you like.

Make it safe

When you make an offer in your marketing, address fears and objections and then offer some kind of guarantee. Managing objections will be discussed in more detail in Chapter 17. Guarantees can vary from how much money you make statements to suggestions about what can be achieved or avoided if the potential client participates in your service. The important thing is to ensure that it is a real guarantee and it feels genuine to your potential client.

Use a variety of methods to build and maintain relationships

We all have preferred styles of marketing, the method we are most comfortable with, but I cannot stress enough that marketing is not about us; it is about our potential clients. Our preferred method may not be theirs, and one method certainly won't reach all of our potential clients. Sticking with what you like has the potential to sabotage your business.

"On average 5 times as many people read the headline as read the body."

David Ogilvy

In all written forms of marketing a few key principles apply. Perhaps the most important is to use a catchy headline, one that grabs attention and enables the audience to self-select. It also needs to deliver the complete message, because 80% won't read beyond it – although at the same time the header should draw the reader into the body of the text. One of the best ways to get the hang of this is to keep reading what other successful people are doing, particularly those whose values reflect your own.

Email

Email marketing is now one of the most common ways of maintaining contact with potential clients. In addition to catchy headers you will need to build a reputation for sending interesting emails, ones that add value, give information or are humorous and entertaining. In Chapter 9 we discussed measuring marketing activity; email and online activity are perhaps the easiest forms to measure. What you are looking for is the general level of interest – how many people opened the email; the subject-specific interest – what links people clicked on; and your unsubscribe rate. Most of the basic and free CRM systems will do this kind of tracking for you, enabling you to see what works, what to repeat and what to discard.

Website

Having a website is considered crucial by many coaches – but if you look at what these sites are delivering in terms of marketing and business growth, the results are negligible. If you want your site to work for you, there are some fundamentals that you need to consider. The site's purpose is in part to showcase your offering, but mostly to attract business, so there should be some way for your clients to link with you other than by filling in a 'contact us' form. One option is to offer some free information by way of a report or a video in exchange for an email address. This way you can start to build up a relationship with prospective clients, rather than have them wander onto your site and off it again and with you being none the wiser. For those of you grimacing at the idea of collecting emails and thinking your potential clients will go elsewhere … relax. This may have been the case five years ago, but not now. People are very used to putting their email address into websites, it's no big deal. In fact, if the person on your site will not exchange their email address for your valuable information about something they're considering, they're unlikely to buy anyway, so you've lost nothing.

Make sure that you have control over your website and can make text changes when you need to. Keep the site simple and use landing pages for marketing activity. As far as search engine optimisation (SEO) is concerned, you need to understand the very basics, such as your website analytics, how to use keywords and online keyword tools. For anything more sophisticated, if you're really interested then learn about it; otherwise, outsource it to someone who knows what they are doing. They will do a better job in a fraction of the time you'd spend.

Video

Using video is a great way to engage with your potential clients on a more personal basis: it's easy to do and you can upload files to sites such as YouTube. Remember to stick to your message, understand your clients' perspective and make them feel that you really know what they need and where they're coming from.

Social media

Using social media is also increasingly important in your online profile, and you can be sure that potential clients will take a look to get to know you better. Make sure that your social media, if linked to your business, reflects what you want people to see of you, and that your profiles are up to date.

Blogging is a great way to stay in touch with your clients and your potential market, as well as to maintain your online profile. Write about the things you want to be found for, have an aim in mind, a message you want to share when you write a blog, and make sure that you promote it through your social media networks.

Advertising

Advertising in journals, trade magazines and papers does have its place, but it is generally costly, so be sure that you know what your return on the investment is. Make sure the publication you advertise in is very targeted towards the clients you want and that you have a reply code or discrete URL so that you can track how many enquiries you get from a specific advert. Just because your ad is in print, don't be tempted to write it and leave it to run repeatedly for months, particularly in a subscription publication. It quickly becomes wallpaper and your potential clients won't see it. Change the headline, offers and layout regularly so that people notice your advert. As you track the results over a number of months you'll identify which ones are working best and you can start to model future campaigns around them.

Testimonials

Testimonials provide excellent social proof and you should be asking your clients for them as a matter of course. They should follow a structure that enables potential clients to understand what you do and how you have helped previous clients (Box 10.1).

Box 10.1: Testimonial template

- Previous situation
- Name
- Problem
- What was done
- Result
- Benefit
- Emotion/feeling

Example

Before I met Richard from Appraisal360 I knew that I needed a 360° feedback solution for the NHS but had no idea how to set it up.

Richard helped me to create the right competences in a simple, easy-to-use online system that my clients love. I now have the flexibility to create bespoke 360 questionnaires in a fast and cost-effective way, without having to worry about complex technology.

Marketing requires time, attention and effort, and about 80% of the time it won't work as well as you'd hoped. This said, it is the most important activity in business growth. If your clients don't know about you, they won't buy from you.

CHAPTER 11

Know your niche

In our industry having a niche is currently one of the most talked-about business development topics. If it's so important, why aren't we all niching like mad? Is having a niche really a help – or just a load of hype? When I talk to clients about identifying their niche they almost always get the philosophy, and they understand why having a niche makes marketing so much easier. But when it comes to applying niching principles to their own business, the matter becomes a whole lot more scary. In many ways it may appear counterintuitive; if you're trying to find more clients, why would you exclude those who don't fit with your niche? If you want to grow your business, why would you shrink your potential market?

The reality is that it's a whole lot more scary not to have a niche, as far as marketing is concerned. A niche enables you to connect with a specific group of people in a much more meaningful way; it allows you to target your marketing messages towards that group; and it enables you to stand out from the crowd. When you consider the big, successful brands, they almost all have a target group of clients and a niche message for those clients. For example, compare Volvo and BMW. They actually provide a similar range of products: mid-range to high-end cars aimed at the more affluent driver. From there they have each developed very different niche identities or target people for their marketing, and different client groups who have become their loyal fans. Would the majority of BMW drivers – looking for style, performance and luxury – go for the Volvo – for safety, low environmental impact and design? Probably not.

The same can be said of successful hair product brands: Head & Shoulders for dandruff, John Frieda's Sheer Blonde for blondes, and so on. Do other companies make hair products for these groups of people? Of course they do, but being known for a specific area of the market gives a company the edge. It's no different in coaching. What you are known for and who you work with matters in terms of credibility and ease of marketing.

There are three components to your niche: the topic you cover, the actual niche and your identity (Figure 11.1).

Figure 11.1: The three components of your niche

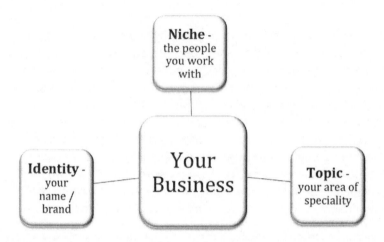

These have a dependent relationship. For example, if you have a very tight topic you can afford to have a much broader niche. Appriasal360 has a very tight topic: it offers online 360° feedback solutions. It can therefore have a wider industry niche. On the other hand, if you have a broad topic, like learning and development, you need to offer it to a narrower niche. The case study below reflects how niching can be developed.

Case study 10: Niching

Claire set up her business as a Reiki healer after she had been made redundant. She was already qualified and provided therapy for friends and family; now she needed to find some paying clients – and fast. Her Uncle Dave was a local businessman who had a small garage out of which he did bodywork and car repairs. He advised Claire to advertise in the local free paper and told her she'd soon get going. After four weeks, two phone calls and no clients Claire decided that a different strategy might be needed. She came to see me for a one-off strategy session.

We talked through Claire's action so far, identified what she wanted to achieve and set about designing a plan. One of her challenges was the number of Reiki healers in the area, so we looked at how Claire could stand out. In complete contrast to what her Uncle had advised, we considered how Claire could niche her service, where she would find her clients and how she could best fulfil their needs. Claire said that most of the friends who had used her service were single women and that a lot them felt stressed. So we put a few lifestyle indicators around a Reiki package and created a specialist service for stressed-out single women. A year later Claire has a waiting list for appointments, commands some of the highest fees in the area and is thoroughly enjoying her business.

The reason why Claire is so successful is that she identified a tight niche in a crowded market. It is, therefore, much easier for her to stand out.

Identity is the third component of niching. This can be your brand's synergy with your product or service – there are plenty of examples of both small and large businesses that use this principle. For example, several dentists have practices near where I live and all of them offer teeth whitening. One dentist advertises himself as 'The Smile Maker'. He specialises in teeth whitening and cosmetic dentistry to give you the smile you want. His identity says what he does; it gives him a niche and makes him a specialist in that niche, not just a dentist. The result is that he's the 'go to' man for teeth whitening, he finds the clients he wants more easily and he can charge a premium.

Your name also works as an identity draw if you are well known in your industry. Take Tony Robbins, for example. His name is his brand and those of us in the people development field automatically equate him with NLP and personal growth. This means that his topic and niche will be less important to his business. The same could have been said of Anita Roddick. Many people did business with The Body Shop because of what she stood for and her personal values. This gave her a specific identity in the market; which, in turn, created a group of followers with similar values on which marketing could be based. Unless you have celebrity status in your industry, identity is perhaps the least critical component of the three; the relationship between topic and niche is most critical. However, a very clear brand name or personal identity will further clarify who your marketing is aimed at and allow your customers to self-select, to some degree.

When we choose a product or service we make our decision based on emotion. Much of the positive emotion needed to get a client to choose you depends on rapport, creating a feeling of sameness or that the person they are buying from understands them and what they need or want. Hence topic and niche become important because successful marketing strategy is focused on meeting the needs or solving the problems of a specific group. It is much easier to build the relationship once they identify with you and start to feel comfortable with you.

While building relationships with people and gaining their trust takes time and work, it is also worth remembering that much of our decision making is emotional and intuitive, and can happen in an instant. In Blink, Malcolm Gladwell describes a two second rapid cognition in which we make decisions about people we meet, about things we may buy, and the books we like etc. He says this is powerful and important. It is a type of rational thinking based on our experiences to date. Our brain finds points of reference that can quickly determine whether a product, service, person or business is the right fit for us. So if people are looking to experience, values and emotion to make their decisions, whether rapidly or over a period of time, the ability to engage with potential clients on an emotional and experiential basis is critical to marketing success. This is much easier to achieve when you have a specific focus, such as a problem, a group of people or a specific value.

Choosing a niche

Choosing a niche doesn't commit you for life; it doesn't mean you can't follow any other passions and dreams; and you are not restricted to operating in one niche only. In fact you may find several niche groups of clients within the topic area you work in. The key is that your niche determines your marketing messages and customer acquisition; having a targeted message for a specific group of potential clients is much more effective than having a catch-all message that actually engages no one. If you have multiple niche areas, treat them like discrete businesses as far as marketing is concerned and target the specific issues for each group. Not doing so really does sabotage your success.

Your niche allows you to be a specialist, which is always more popular with clients. It allows you to work with people who you know and understand; it enables you to really get to their motivations, their pain, their values, and the outcomes that they are looking for when they consider using your services. You can focus on these things to create interest and value around the issues that matter to your chosen group. As you develop your credibility in your chosen niche customers will find you.

While this can feel a bit overwhelming to the generalist coach who takes whatever work comes along, there are some tips for success, and some tried and tested components to a good niche. If you have an established business, the best place to start is with your existing clients. If you are new to business, you may want to start with the components of a good niche (see below).

Exercise 4: Identifying your niche from your existing clients

Take a cold, hard look at whom you currently do business with and ask yourself the following questions:

1. Who are my best-paying clients?
2. Who do I most enjoy working with?
3. What are the commonalities between these different clients?
4. Who do I not enjoy working with?
5. What common traits do these people have?

Once you have identified the commonalities between your best customers, then seek to really understand them.

Demographics:

1. Do they fit within a specific age bracket?
2. Is there a gender bias?
3. Where are they located?
4. Are there specific lifestyle traits?
5. Is there a typical economic profile?
6. Are they employed, business owners, not working, students?
7. What do they read, watch and listen to?

Psychographics:

1. Values and beliefs
2. Goals / aspirations
3. Fears
4. Common behaviours
5. Decision making patterns

Once you understand the profile of your best clients it is both easier and less scary to build a niche around them. As a result of profiling them much more closely you will know who and where they are, what drives them, what they fear most and what they want. You will then be able to create marketing activities specifically to attract the clients you most want. You go to places where they are; you ensure that you or your service is visible in the places where they look, whether online, in print or face to face; and you attract them to your business with a compelling outcome that fits with their desires and emotional pull. This makes you stand out as the person who understands them. Your ability to create a niche that works depends largely on the amount of effort you are prepared to put into understanding your clients, identifying the ones you want to work with and taking action to get known by those potential clients.

There are some key components to a good niche, and it is worth working through these before committing yourself to a particular group. These basic elements will help you to decide if your niche is viable as a business. Many people believe that a niche has to be unique, or so different that only you can provide it. This is vanity. In most niches there will be competition, variants of what you do and consumer choice. This is desirable. You just need to know what it is that makes you stand out. In fact, in many cases a niche where no one else operated would raise concerns about the viability of the market.

Components of a good niche

You are passionate about the area or client group

Box 11.1: Components of a good niche

1. You are passionate about the area or client group
2. Your have some expertise / knowledge in your chosen area
3. You have contacts in your chosen niche
4. There is a market for what you are offering
5. It is an accessible niche
6. It has a transformative value for clients
7. There are people willing to pay for what you do.

Your enthusiasm, energy and passion are a vital part of your marketing; you need to capture your clients' imagination and emotion. This often means spending a considerable amount of time with your chosen niche – the people, the subject and the values. You must like being with that group, have some passion for the stuff they need and enjoy solving their problems.

You have some expertise/knowledge in your chosen area

A thorough knowledge of the subject area and the issues facing your potential clients, together with experience in the field, are very powerful motivators for clients to choose you. Your expertise allows you to use the same niche language; this is particularly important for coaches working in specific industry sectors or with specific professional groups. Experience of similar life events, such as redundancy, illness, bankruptcy, divorce or trauma, enables you to connect with clients at a deeper level and to create the trust, familiarity and confidence that they need in order to do business with you.

You have contacts in your chosen niche

Lots of my clients find that their best customers come from areas they know well, often because they have worked in the field prior to setting up their own people development business. One of the main benefits of this is that they have plenty of contacts in the field. This makes business acquisition easier. If you leave a particular field because you hate it, then this is not the place to establish your niche, however many contacts you may have. If you move on from a profession, industry or activity that you love for other reasons, you are probably better placed than most coaches to provide services to that group. Use this to make yourself stand out.

Case study 11: Expertise and contacts

Andy is a good example of niching in an area where you have both expertise and contacts. He is a teacher by professional background who now teaches conflict resolution techniques. Andy doesn't teach conflict resolution to anyone, like many trainers; he has carved himself a niche working with teachers in secondary schools. Andy has worked his many contacts and is not short of work in his chosen area. This is mostly because he understands where his clients are coming from, the constraints that teachers face in managing conflict, and the things that cause them distress – and he speaks their language, which gives them confidence that the solutions he offers will work for them.

Ensure there is a market for what you are offering

Do your homework. Be sure that there are enough potential customers in your niche area for you to build a business from them.

Ensure that your potential market is accessible

Make sure that you can get your product and service in front of your potential market relatively easily and cheaply. A good way of knowing that you can do this is to do your profiling homework (Exercise 4). Once you understand where your clients are and what they are reading it's much easier to find ways of getting in front of them. Think about networks both online and face to face; trade publications as well as local ones if relevant. Also consider shows, conferences and appropriate social media.

Offer transformational value to your clients

Your product or service will make a big difference to your clients' lives. Identify where it makes a difference – this is usually in terms of outcome. This may be a real benefit, such as making money, having more time, a better lifestyle; or it may be pain avoidance, such as reducing worry, hassle, fear or preventing something negative from happening for a client. Be very clear about what transformational value you bring in your marketing.

Have a service that clients are willing to pay for

This can often be as simple as identifying what your clients want over what they need. Something that is wanted is often perceived as being more valuable than something that is needed. Coffee is a good example here. You only have to observe people coming to work at any large office block: they walk in clinging to their big paper cups containing various versions of Costa or Starbucks coffee to get them started for the morning. Could they get a coffee once they got to work? Of course they could – but they're prepared to pay a premium for the coffee shop version they want. Get to know your niche well; understand what they want. If you can't identify a want, make sure that you have a market. Be creative though and, if possible, create some want around your clients' needs.

Whatever niche you choose, spend time understanding it, work the contacts you already have and make yourself known within your niche. This will allow you to build relationships with potential clients, helping them to choose your business over another.

Your niche gives you clarity of message, which enables you to communicate effectively and take targeted action to promote the value of your product or service.

CHAPTER 12
Positioning yourself

Positioning is about where you place yourself in your chosen market. Positioning in the market is influenced by many different things, including branding, price, quality and expertise. There is plenty of evidence to show that experts command higher fees, get clients more easily and have more opportunities. So if you have your own business, being an expert in your field is a no-brainer – isn't it? Once you have identified your niche, the next step is to establish yourself as an expert in that area.

The fact is that in most professions – and people development is no different – most people in the industry are average performers. Some are poor performers and some are excellent. Being excellent takes knowledge, practice and focus, as we discussed in Chapter 5. Being an expert certainly requires a degree of personal excellence. It needs the right mindset to keep you on track and it requires certain behaviours and skill sets, which are described below.

The reality is that being an expert is relative to the people you are with. You could easily find yourself an expert on your subject in one group of people and a relative novice in another. If you look back over your childhood and young adulthood you can often find examples of this. For me, it was playing chess at school. I was captain of the school team, had an unbeaten record during my last school year and led the team to victory in the regional schools' competition even though we were rank outsiders. I considered myself to be something of an expert. Then I started to play with people in my university club and the local chess group, and I discovered that once again I was a novice by comparison. I also discovered that I didn't have the passion or the persistence to continue to develop my chess skills at this level. I still play occasionally, and I enjoy it – but an expert I am not.

Defining what an expert is can be an interesting exercise in itself. Some say it is knowing more than anyone else on a given subject, others say you need a lifetime of experience in your chosen field. Essentially, you are an expert if you have specialist skills or knowledge in a particular subject or field. If you analyse this further by looking at the skills people have, you can see that it's actually not difficult to be a bona fide expert in several areas of your life – and most people have at least one area in which they have specific expertise. It's what you do with that expertise that determines how you might benefit from it in your work life.

Most of the business development and marketing literature around today promotes the need to be an expert if you want success, and to a large degree this is true. Too often though, marketing literature oversimplifies what is required. Being an expert isn't just about completing a series of actions that get your message out, it's about having genuine credibility and, most importantly, the self-belief to support the expert status.

If we look at our own industry, people developers are being encouraged to find a niche and be an expert. That's pretty much what I'm saying to you here, right? Well, not really. I believe that there is a lot of work going into creating the impression of expertise – such as writing e-books, clever branding, copycat tactics and public speaking. I'm not knocking any of these activities, they are all important steps in the journey to being an expert. Each one of them raises your profile and gets you noticed both by your potential clients and within your industry. While this is always desirable, it's not enough. None of this by itself will get you expert status.

It is part of the journey, but without the effort and investment in yourself this level of exposure is not sustainable, it's not credible beyond a superficial level and it's not very satisfying for the 'expert' concerned.

Box 12.1: Metrics of a real expert

1. **Competency** - delivers real value to the client.
2. **Respected** - by peers and others in own industry.
3. **Qualified to teach others** - both from a perspective of expertise and knowledge, academic qualifications can give further credibility but they are not the only indicator.
4. **Authority** - known in field and shares knowledge and thoughts.
5. **Fees** - reflect degree of expertise.

How to become a real expert

Becoming an expert requires work. It doesn't just happen, it develops over time. The time-frame varies hugely from one individual to another. If you consider Malcolm Gladwell's book *Outliers* – he found plenty of evidence to support the view that an expert had about 10,000 hours of experience in their chosen specialism. That's somewhere between 10 and 20 years for most of us, and certainly much longer than most business owners can afford to spend acquiring their status. Of course the time required to acquire expertise really depends on how hard you are prepared to work at it and what action you take.

Box 12.2: Becoming an expert

1. Pick a topic.
2. Cultivate breadth and depth.
3. Share your knowledge.
4. Intentional practice.

Pick a topic

This is very similar to choosing your niche – and of course the two are completely interdependent. Your topic should be something you are passionate about, something you enjoy learning about, talking about and working with. As discussed in Part 1 (see Step 5), this will help you through the tough times when it seems like more pain than gain. When you pick your topic, be sure to narrow it down sufficiently. It's difficult to achieve the metrics of an expert if the subject area is too broad. It's also important to choose a topic that has a big enough market for you to stand out as an expert.

Case study 12: Choosing the right topic

I worked with John a few years ago. He wanted to leave his NHS career and set up as a consultant. John had a clinical background in emergency care and had spent some time teaching clinical skills and a short time in management. At the time, emergency care reform was a very political issue, emergency care services were under a lot of scrutiny and there was demand for external consultants to support the reform agenda. John found some associate work through his contacts in the field, shared his specialist knowledge and was very quickly working at capacity and making double what he'd been earning in the NHS.

After about a year, John and I did some work on the direction his business should take. John said he wasn't really happy and didn't enjoy the work enough to justify the amount of time he was spending away from his young family. He felt trapped because his family had got used to the income and he didn't want to let them down, but he felt that he couldn't carry on with the consultancy work.

John had chosen to work in an area where he already had some expertise, but what he hadn't done was narrow that area down enough. He hadn't identified what he was really passionate about, or identified how he could work just in the area of emergency care. As a result, he hadn't created an identity that was narrow enough to give him credibility with the clients he wanted to work with; or one that would make him stand out in the area of emergency care he was passionate about.

When we did some work to explore John's real passion we found it was in emergency care – but not in consultancy and systems reform. So when the trade-off, between the role and money verses time away from his family, was assessed the reward was not enough. What John was really passionate about was the standard of clinical skills amongst emergency care staff, and how this could literally make the difference between patients living and dying in the initial stages of emergency care. John was a real clinical expert, he had taught this subject for several years and really missed the buzz it gave him. He didn't believe that anyone would pay him to teach clinical skills because there were many courses were already provided by academic establishments. In other words his self limiting belief put him in his own way.

After exploring whether these establishments had his expertise in the field, and whether there was an on-going need in the health service for this type of training, John started to form a plan. He developed a specialist clinical skills course, focused on local needs and delivered by a true expert in the subject. He soon had some bookings, and he has maintained his business for several years now, despite changing political agendas and economic constraints. This work pattern also allowed him to be with his family more and, because of the way training is provided, he could pre-plan when he was away further in advance. John's success has been significantly aided by his expertise in a narrow field and his ability to identify the outcomes required in the field and then to position his service accordingly. John has maintained his success more easily because he has a topic that he is passionate about, he enjoys learning about it himself and he can talk forever about the subject.

Cultivate breadth and depth

Being a genuine expert is work in progress. You never arrive at expertise and stop; there is always more to learn – and you often know more than you think you do. The journey to becoming an expert is one where you are constantly seeking out information in your subject. Learn about your topic, research what others are doing in your field. This allows you to mingle confidently with your peers and earn their respect. It gives you something to discuss and talk or write about.

Find established experts in your field, people you respect, look up to and are happy to use as role models. Build relationships with them, learn from them and share your thoughts with them. Most are more than willing to talk about their work and their passion, particularly if you are writing about it or passing the information on in a manner that credits them.

Join groups of people who are interested in your subject, both face-to-face and online. Spending time with people who are interested in your topic helps you to develop your thinking, challenge any assumptions you may have made and clarify your marketing messages. It is also a great way to get known within your peer group and find opportunities to excel.

Take courses and classes if you need to, but know when enough is enough. Don't confuse perpetual education with becoming an expert – it is far more likely to be procrastination caused by a boundary condition. You, like all experts, are work in progress – you don't need to have all your ducks in a row before you start to engage with peers or potential clients.

Finally – and I cannot stress this enough – read, read, read. Know what is current and topical, read books, and also blogs, trade magazines – both those specific to your industry and to your intended clients – and follow the news relating to your topic. Read stuff written by recognised experts in your subject and that of newcomers. Comment on what you read, engage with others in your field and get yourself known.

Share your knowledge

Get recognised by your peer group and your potential market. If you have done the groundwork above, it is likely that you have moved beyond the level of superficial knowledge that makes exposure unsustainable. You are ready to get out there, to keep growing and to start reaping the rewards from the effort you have put in so far. So start to share your knowledge. Get talking about your topic whenever the opportunity arises.

Start to write about your subject. Having your own blog is a great way to get your message out. If writing is not your thing, make some videos and post them; it has never been easier to share your work. As well as writing on your own forums, offer articles to trade journals, information for publication or display in places where your customers go, and make sure that what you put out is valuable to your potential clients. Share information and things that will help your potential clients and your peers don't just promote yourself or attempt to sell.

Speaking has two purposes. The first and main one is to get in front of potential clients and give them a good-quality experience and weave in information about what you can do for them. The second is to build your expert status by getting in front of your peers and other authorities in your field, so offer to speak at your own industry events too. Being known and credible opens up a huge amount of opportunity.

Intentional practice

When you consider any experts in their field, whether intellectual, physical or skills driven, they all practise. The nearer they are to the top of their game, the more time they spend on practice. This is also true for aspiring experts. It is not enough to be involved with your topic, or interested in what's going on. To become an expert, you have to take specific, targeted action towards that end. You have to learn and to practise, regularly and repeatedly.

Dr K. Anders Erricson, a leading authority on deliberate (or intentional) practice says that in order to become an expert in anything, it is the way you practise that matters. While Erricson's work was the basis for the 10,000 hours rule mentioned above, he also identifies how deliberate practice can enhance performance through mindset as much as skill set. The sort of practice needed to become an expert needs to be very focused and structured. Each session should have a time-frame, a goal and a measure for success. Lessons learned from the practice session can be applied and the process repeated, again and again, focusing on developing the areas where there is most to be gained.

Box 12.3: Intentional practice

- Time-frame
- Goal
- Measure for results
- Lessons learned
- What next?

The key here is the same, whether you are an athlete, a musician or an industry expert; constantly renew your experiences, challenge yourself a little more and learn from what you do. This way you will continually raise your game and grow. If you don't take this approach, you run the risk of repeating the same experience over and over, and this keeps you at your existing skill level and prevents you from developing real expertise. Practice can be hard work and this is where your passion for your topic really supports you. Your passion helps you to enjoy the practice more – and to stick at it when you're not enjoying it so much. Passion for the topic also means that you enjoy the progress, get satisfaction from your achievement and create energy and drive for the next challenge.

As an expert, you can present yourself to your potential clients with confidence, credibility and authority. Because you know your subject so well, it is easier to know your market well and to apply all of the niching behaviours discussed above. As an expert, you can confidently write on your subject, offer advice and value to your potential clients, engage with the media on topical issues and speak at your own or others' events. To be an expert, you have to put in the effort, the practice and the time to establish yourself. This gives you the substance to support the public persona that sustains your business.

As you work towards being an expert, establish your differences as well as your credibility. This is how you stand out. Most importantly, be yourself: let your personality show, be unique and authentic, let your values, drivers and what you stand for shine through. Learn from others and have role models, but establish your own style or way and don't be tempted just to copy. Finally, when you have earned credibility in your field, be prepared to be defined by your ideas and your actions and to command the fees that you are worth.

CHAPTER 13
The sales funnel

The final part of your business model is to know your sales funnel. This is the way in which you move people from first knowing about you to becoming your paying clients. Really understanding how this process works can make a significant difference to the profitability of your business. The sales funnel is about numbers (see Tables 9.1 and 9.2 above). It is a way of understanding how to get enough people buying from you - how you can increase the number of people buying from you and the amount they spend with you, and how to ensure repeat business.

> *"Once you see the funnel it is easy to see how valuable your existing customers are."*

Seth Godin

As its name suggests, your sales funnel has a wide opening, or entry point, at the top, allowing people to enter from multiple places. As you move down the funnel it narrows, but the value increases, so that those who make it to the bottom of the funnel are your high-value clients (Figure 13.1).

13.1 Sales funnel

Your sales funnel should be treated as a process for mapping how people do business with you. It gives you knowledge and understanding of what is happening with your clients, what they like, what they will

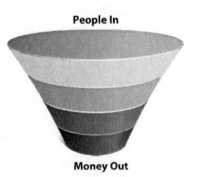

People In

Money Out

pay for and where they might leave your sales process. It is a tried and tested strategy that has been used in most industry sectors over many years. In the people development industry, it's easy to recognise the funnel in action in most of the successful businesses. It demands planning, monitoring, measuring and changing if necessary, but it will deliver results when you put the effort into building a funnel for your business and understanding how it is working for you.

How to build a good sales funnel

To build a good sales funnel, you need to know what you want to come out of the bottom, or, as Steven Covey more eloquently says, to 'start with the end in mind'. Understand what the high-value product or service that you sell is; know how much of it you need to sell in order to achieve what you want; and know what sort of people your high-value clients are. Then build both upwards and downwards through your funnel to ensure that you have the right value and products in place to achieve your end (Figure 13.2).

13.2 The sales funnel at work

People who become aware of your service

multiple leads in

give free information — Build relationship and create value

low cost item — Low risk purchase

create upsell — Increase client value

high cost — High profit product

Profit

Case study 13: Oprah Winfrey's funnel

To demonstrate the above process, it's worth looking at well-established, successful business funnels. In 2011, Oprah Winfrey, the queen of daytime TV, was reported to be worth over $2.7 billion. She has achieved this through multiple revenue streams and massive action towards her goal. While the funnel illustrated in Figure 13.3 is oversimplified, it does give an indication of how she has leveraged her expertise and profile to create a huge revenue stream.

Figure 13.3: Oprah Winfrey's sales funnel

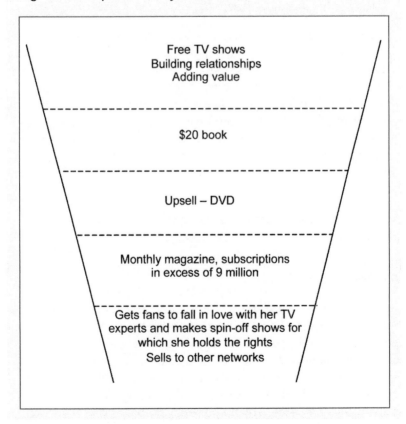

At the top of Oprah's funnel is her daily presence on TV, which gave her fans and potential clients the opportunity to get great value from her for free and to build relationships with her.

She used her shows to create a sense of well-being for potential clients and she shared a lot of valuable information through her guest experts – also for free. She now has millions of viewers – who are potential clients – engaged with what she's saying.

She then makes a low-cost offer of a $20 book, followed by offering an upsell of a DVD to those who buy the book.

To build a sustained, passive income, Oprah next builds a subscription-based monthly magazine into the funnel. Over 9 million of her fans have bought it.

Then comes the really clever part. Although her daily show finished in 2011, her Oprah Winfrey Network (OWN) continues to produce daily programmes targeted at the same demographic group. Oprah used this fan base, her clients' loyalty, to create a number of spin-off shows featuring her experts, the people whom she has made her fans fall in love with. She creates these shows, for which she holds the production rights, and then sells them on as her high-ticket item to other networks.

In order to build your funnel, you need to focus on the outcome of your activity at each stage of the client journey.

Awareness

People can be exposed to your service or product in many different ways, and it is easy for you to get lost in the crowd of other products and services on offer. You need to have a purposeful online presence. This doesn't mean a static, brochure website that is visited only by people you have given the web address to. Your online presence may be a website; or it may be your blog or your social media presence. The purpose of your online presence is to collect leads and build relationships and trust, so make sure that this is what you convey. Also ensure that your potential clients can contact you both online and offline.

Box 13.1: Routes into your sales funnel

- E-mail marketing
- YouTube
- Social media
- Google and other search engines
- Direct mail
- Joint ventures
- Conferences
- Face-to-face meetings
- Telesales
- Webinars

Lead generation

Once you have decided what you want to achieve, you need a strategy for getting people who have become aware of you to engage with you and give you permission to send them information. This is called a lead generator. A very effective way to use a lead generator is through a landing page (also called a squeeze page). This is a web page, usually separate from your main website, where people can download your free information in exchange for their contact details. Once you have their details, you can continue to move some of these people down your funnel by providing more value and information. All of this occurs before any attempt at selling or overtly promoting your product has taken place. It is your opportunity to establish your credibility and expertise. The kinds of things you can offer are reports, e-books, top tips, buying guides, strategies, a quick fix for a problem your clients are likely to have. Any information that you provide, whether written or video, should be well presented, relevant to the client group and show you in a good light.

Low-risk purchase

From here you can offer a low-risk purchase opportunity. This may be a book, an MP3 podcast or a CD, or a seminar place. You are essentially testing the relationship so far, checking that you have offered the right value content to move your prospects on to become paying clients. If you have planned your funnel well you will have an idea of the number of clients that you need at this stage, and each stage through the funnel, to ensure you have enough clients at the end of your funnel to achieve your aim. If you haven't generated as much interest as you would have liked, go back up the funnel and check that you have enough of the right people coming into it and that you are offering enough targeted value to make them take action.

The upsell

This is the part of the funnel where you increase your client value. Places like McDonald's are masters at this; you go in to order a burger and they ask you if you want fries, or you order a meal and they ask you to 'go large'. The cost difference per individual customer is very small, but when this happens thousands of time an hour around the globe the cost-benefit to McDonald's is huge.

The trick here is to make it easy for clients to buy from you. Offer a cheap product to get them in the buying mood. This must still be something that the client wants and that has a high perceived value to them. Then offer something that complements what they have bought, builds depth or offers a different way of experiencing more. Bundles and upgrades are great ways to upsell. If you think about budget airlines; it's actually quite difficult to come away only having paid for your seat, with the number of options and upsells available it's likely that one of them will be a 'necessity' or compelling enough want for many of us to buy.

The kind of things that coaches can put in their upsell packages are diagnostic tools, workbooks, educational videos, recordings of seminars and bundled coaching sessions at a small discount. When you are designing your upsell keep an eye on your profit margins and ensure you are increasing client profitability – don't just do more work for similar profit. Your upsell can include a range of products that also sell in their own right on your website.

Passive income

Membership sites and subscription-based services are a great way to build regular monthly income. There are plenty of online tools that allow you to provide these kinds of services easily. They are a great addition to your funnel if you have followers who would enjoy a more structured interaction with you. They are also good for running shorter training programmes. Clients subscribe for a set length of time and have access to all the necessary training materials; then, at the end of their training period, they are offered an extension if they want it.

High-value programme

This is where you make most of your profit. It may be your flagship coaching programme, leadership development or some kind of 'do it for you' service. There are two key considerations here. The first is not to constrain your potential by committing to too much 'time for money' activity. For example, where possible, opt for group activity, not one-to-one. Where your high-value service is one-to-one, ensure that you have other revenue streams to sustain growth. All activity through your sales funnel should be directed towards keeping as many of the right clients in the funnel so as to ensure that you can sell enough of your high-value product or service.

Used properly, a well-designed sales funnel will help you to organise your marketing activity, identify what works and focus your activity. It is worth spending time to map this out properly, to implement it and to measure the outcomes of activity all along the way – but particularly in terms of what lead generation is working best, to enable you to do more.

Growing your business

This chapter and Chapters 9, 10, 11 and 12 have focused on your business and the skill set you need to ensure that you are able to grow your business the way you want to. Marketing is a critical part of any successful business. It should be treated both as a science, with robust testing and measuring, and as an art, with imagination and creativity. It takes time and practice to get the formula right. Good marketing strategies develop out of knowing your target market really well, understanding their pain, their fears and their wants. Good marketing also positions you as an expert with your target clients. It enables you to speak their language, builds trust into the relationship and helps your target clients to feel that you really understand them and can offer the outcome they are looking for.

To be able to achieve these things most easily it's necessary for you to have a niche area in which you work predominantly. It's worth spending time to identify what this niche is and how you relate to it. Most people have a niche type of client in their business already, and almost all of us have an 'ideal' client. This is a good place to start when choosing who to work with. It informs how to position yourself as an expert, and how to design your sales funnel.

CHAPTER 14

360 Feedback As A Business Generating Tool

Why use a tool or product?

For many people developers one of the biggest challenges in getting business from larger clients is having a product they are looking for, clearly packaged in a way that meets their immediate 'need'. To the client, this need or problem might look quite different from the solutions a consultant or coach may offer. Frequently, clients already have an idea of what 'solution' they want and go looking for that, not necessarily for a coach or consultant. Many of us in the people development industry don't help ourselves by creating products and brands with complex or artfully vague names and explanations. This makes it difficult for a new client to engage with us, or to buy from us because they don't really understand what the outcome will be for them. Offering a tool or product that is well known and understood is a great door opener. The challenge is to ensure you make it your own, so that you stand out. You can do this either by adapting the well-known product to your specific market or by building a package of support around it that demonstrates your unique expertise.

Chapters 14 and 15 use 360 feedback as an example of how a well known product can fit into your sales funnel and help you attract more of the clients you want.

The principle can be adapted to work with any number of development tools, training packages or consultancy services. I know it sounds too simple, but by linking your offering to a recognisable requirement the client has - such as well-known personality profiling or team building tools that you are accredited to use, or hanging your offer on the back of statutory training you deliver, (like health and safety or accredited leadership courses) –

and then putting your own niche or expert spin on them, you can get through doors that would have otherwise stayed closed.

I have chosen 360 feedback to demonstrate this process because I know it works, I used it to build my own business, and I have worked with many clients who use it as part of their business.

What is 360° feedback?

360° feedback is a process whereby an individual receives feedback on their performance from a number of people with whom they work closely and who know them well enough to comment on their behaviours and skills.

The individual seeking feedback (the appraisee) typically completes a self-perception questionnaire and then asks around 8–10 other people to provide their own feedback using the same set of questions. This is most easily facilitated using an online system such as Appraisal360. The people giving feedback (the respondents) are usually arranged into groups depending on the relationship they have to the appraisee; for example, senior, peer, junior and client. This gives the appraisee a much more rounded picture of their performance and their impact on other people. This can be particularly valuable in complex organisations where the appraisee is part of several teams or works autonomously and the line manager may not fully understand the contribution they make (CIPD 2011).

The 360° feedback questionnaire usually consists of a set of questions relevant to the appraisee's role. It is an excellent way of measuring behaviour and interpersonal skills as well as role-specific functions. However, 360° feedback is not always the best way of measuring hard performance targets and very technical competencies where there is only a right or wrong way of doing things.

The best way to collect 360° feedback is to use a scale with which people are familiar – for example, the Likert scale, a graded response scale such as 1–5 scoring with a description of what each number means and a 'don't know' option. Within the 360 questionnaire respondents should also have the opportunity to provide free-text comments.

This information is compiled into a report that shows the average feedback for each competency area and the actual scores for each behaviour measured, as well as any free-text comments. The report should be clear enough for the appraisee to understand and use it unaided. However, 360° feedback is much more powerful when the outcomes of the report are considered in a facilitated feedback session. This is where a coach, consultant or learning and development specialist trained in 360° feedback can add real value to the 360 process.

Figure 14.1 shows what you can expect from 360° feedback. You put in information from groups of people who you work regularly with, and you can expect to get back a report that describes your self-awareness, impact, performance and strengths and development areas.

Figure 14.1: 360° feedback

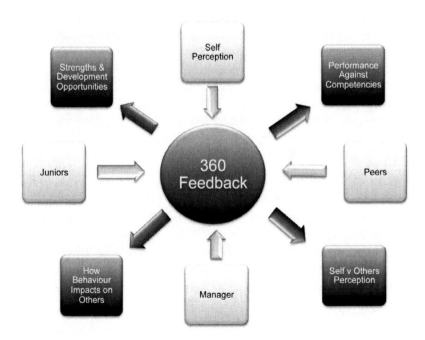

Why use 360° feedback?

Unlike some psychometric interventions, 360° feedback is based on questions relevant to the appraisee's role and it provides real perceptions from real people whose opinions matter to the appraisee. This makes 360° feedback an extremely powerful process for the individual going through it. It is a process that should be undertaken with care, planning and organisational engagement. How to set up an effective 360° feedback project is discussed in detail in Chapter 15.

"360° feedback gives us the opportunity to see ourselves the way others see us."

Richard Oppenheimer

For the appraisee, 360° feedback increases self-awareness; it identifies areas of strength and where small enhancements can make big differences. 360° feedback can also help the appraisee to identify the difference between weaker areas that are not significant to their role, i.e. allowable weaknesses, and weaker areas where some change would have a significant impact, i.e. limiting weaknesses. A properly facilitated feedback meeting allows the appraisee to work through their feedback and form an action plan for their development. This can be both motivating and empowering.

For the organisation, effective 360° feedback identifies team strengths and development needs, and high fliers and individuals who may need extra support. It means that development budgets can be targeted to areas where they will have the greatest impact. Evidence also suggests that 360° feedback is instrumental in reducing sickness, raising staff morale and increasing staff retention (CIPD 2008), therefore demonstrating a tangible bottom-line benefit for organisations.

Box 14.1: Benefits of 360° feedback

For the individual:

- increases self-awareness
- enhances understanding of impact on other people
- enables the appraisee to be more influential
- identifies potential barriers to individual progress
- identifies strengths and areas for development
- identifies alignment with organisational values
- gives opportunity to create development plan
- is both motivating and empowering

For the organisation:

- improves communication
- helps to embed company values and expected levels of competence
- identifies cultural behaviours
- acts as a catalyst for change
- identifies organisational strengths and development needs
- focuses resources for training and development
- identifies high fliers and those who may need extra support

Done well, 360° feedback has enormous benefits for the team or organisation; managed badly, the opposite can occur. Kluger and DeNisi (1996) have researched the impact of 360° feedback interventions for over a decade and they divide the effectiveness of 360° feedback roughly into thirds. Crudely, this equates to:

1. **Top third:** Those who ran a well-facilitated 360 project with individual support and identified organisational learning achieved excellent outcomes, with increased staff morale, better retention and better productivity.

2. **Middle third:** Those who ran their projects well but didn't follow through with individual development or identify and act on organisational learning needs experienced an initial peak in performance that quickly dropped off. The conclusion was that the 360° feedback made no difference.

3. **Bottom third:** This group actually did harm with their 360 interventions. Typically, they never really achieved appraisee engagement in the process, they didn't facilitate feedback - they just issued reports and didn't manage the fear and fallout associated with the feedback results – whether good or bad.

360° feedback as a turnkey business

Simply put, a turnkey business, or 'business in a box', uses an existing model to create business opportunities for others to use. The model can be as tight as a formal franchise, like AutoGlass, where the branding, website, operating procedures and products are already identified for the business owner; alternatively, it can be much more flexible, like Appraisal360, giving the business owner a framework, best practice guidance and product line. The business owner is then free to choose to leverage the existing brand or build on their own brand: either will enable the business owner to develop a service for their own niche area.

360° feedback is a great example of a turnkey business; it provides something tangible and easily understood by corporate clients, it is in high demand and it creates outcomes that identify further work for the coaches and consultants running the 360 projects. This is exactly why Appraisal360 has created a high-quality 360° feedback platform for coaches, consultants and trainers who want to increase their presence in the corporate sector by using 360° feedback.

For their 360° feedback project to have the effectiveness of the top third described above, most organisations need the support of an experienced 360° feedback specialist. This is where it becomes an exciting opportunity for those of us working in people development. Being able to provide a product that the client is already looking for, quantify potential returns and deliver a package of value-add to ensure that the client gets a better outcome with you, definitely creates opportunities that may not otherwise have been there. I've certainly found that many clients, large corporates and small businesses decide on a course of action and then look for a supplier to help them. If they want to do 360° feedback with their team they will most likely look for a 360 provider, like Appraisal360 and contact the sales team; but it is less likely that they will initially go looking for a consultant or coach unless they already know someone who delivers 360° feedback. This is where it is hugely advantageous to belong to a larger network so that you are visible in places where potential clients are looking, and you can position yourself in such a way that clients can identify your specific expertise.

As is the case with most businesses, there is more to success than buying the right online system, and as far as 360° feedback goes the online system you choose is a small but critical part of the process. How you position yourself in the market, how you create organisational engagement, plan your 360 project, manage the feedback and ensure organisational learning are all vital to your success as a 360° feedback specialist and, ultimately, to your ability to gain further work from your 360° feedback clients. This is why the 360° Feedback Formula I teach members of the Appraisal360 Network works.

Case study 14: Winning work through 360 products

Clive is a successful leadership consultant. He works mostly in the health sector, specifically, helping GP practices to develop their leadership teams. One of the local Primary Care Trusts (PCT) wanted some 360° feedback that met doctors' professional requirements and created some scope for leadership development. They went looking for a 360° feedback provider. Because Clive was experienced in both leadership development for GPs and 360° feedback he was the ideal choice for the work. Despite his living locally to the practice concerned, Clive was not known to the PCT because much of his work was in other parts of the UK, therefore he would not have been considered for the work. When the PCT approached me as the 360 provider I directed them to Clive because he is a member of the Appraisal360 Practitioner Network. The 360° feedback identified several areas where leadership skills needed development, just as the PCT had anticipated. For Clive, being able to provide the 360 intervention – and doing it well – resulted in a longer-term contract worth, to date, around £15,000. He is still working with the PCT, providing leadership support and 360° feedback to GP practices in his local area.

The 360° Feedback Formula

The 360° Feedback Formula was created for members of the Appraisal360 Practitioner Network to help them to integrate 360° feedback into their businesses in the most effective way. The 360° Feedback Formula focuses largely on skill set and is designed to stop you from sabotaging your business through lack of direction, poor marketing skills or confusing sales messages. It provides a 'business in a box model' that gives you a tool to introduce to clients and the opportunity to start a conversation around a product, rather than about yourself, which can often be easier. 360° feedback also helps you identify where there may be further work, and then provide your client with evidence to demonstrate that need.

Box 14.2: The 360° Feedback Formula

- Know your client group AND understand how to solve their problem.
- Know that you are an expert in your field.
- Create a 360 product that your clients can relate to.
- Sell your clients an outcome, not a product.

- Understand where 360° feedback fits into your sales funnel and how you profit from it.
- Create a 360 bundle that manages your upsell.
- Use organisational learning from 360° feedback to identify further work.
- Invest in yourself and get help when you need it.

The 360° Feedback Formula gives you a structure for using 360° feedback to help you to get more of the clients you want; to raise your profile and expert status; and to understand what gives you and your business the best return on investment, whether that investment is your money, your time or your emotional energy.

The individual elements of the formula are discussed in more detail in the Chapters 9 and 15. To accelerate your understanding, the following overview is offered.

Know your client group AND understand how to solve their problem

To market successfully, you need to know who your best customers are. These are the people who you enjoy working with and the ones who generate the most of your income. You then need to understand the commonalities between these clients. There will be some - if they are not immediately obvious, look deeper into your clients demographics and psychographics. If you are new to business or don't believe that you have a common group of clients, think about the people who would be your ideal clients if you could choose. You can read more about this in Chapter 11, 'Know your niche'.

Know that you are an expert in your field

This is an interesting concept. When we consider experts, we often think of well-known successful people, or the role models that we have created for ourselves. We are all experts in some area of our lives; to be perceived as an expert by someone you quite simply need to know more than they do. I'm not suggesting that you should claim to be an international guru in a subject that you've only worked with for 12 months; I am saying that being an expert doesn't require you to have all your ducks in a row before you venture out from behind your desk, your laptop, your couch or wherever it is that you make yourself busy (i.e. hide) whenever the next step seems a bit scary. If you have run a few 360 projects and you go into an organisation that has never used 360° feedback before, do you think they see you as an expert? Of course they do! And compared to them, you are an expert. All experts engage in a process of continued learning; this is the only way we can stay at the top of our game. To read more about how to identify your expertise and use it to stand out, go to Chapter 10, 'Positioning yourself'.

Create a 360 product that your clients relate to

One of the key reasons for having products in your sales funnel is to make the decision easy for potential clients when it comes to doing business with you. Having a 360 tool that is perceived to be specific to the group of people you choose to work with and that is a good fit with what they want accelerates their decision making because it creates a feeling of familiarity. It builds rapport because your potential client feels like you really understand them, and that creates trust. You can read more about this in Chapter 15, 'Creating your 360 products'.

Sell your clients an outcome, not a product

People don't buy products, they buy solutions or outcomes, so make sure that this is what you are selling. Be sure that you have understood their pain, what they are aiming to achieve and what might make them question their actions or stop them from buying your product. Purchases are usually made following an emotional decision, so build your solution around the outcomes your clients want so that they can make this emotional engagement. Read more in Chapters 16 and 17, on selling 360° feedback.

Understand where 360° feedback fits into your sales funnel and how you profit from it

Having 360° feedback (or any other tool) in your toolkit is great asset – so long as it is working for you and growing your business, and not the other way around. You need to be sure that your positioning is right, that you understand the profit margins involved and, most importantly, you know what high value business your tools are leading your clients towards, i.e. what's at the bottom of your sales funnel. To learn more about how to create an effective sales funnel, go to Chapter 13.

Create a 360 bundle that manages your upsell

Your clients choose to buy 360° feedback from you rather than directly from an online provider because they want more than an online service. You are doing them a disservice if you don't offer this. To build your bundle, you need to understand your client's pain. If time is an issue, offer an upsell to an administered package or premium service; if cost is an issue, consider group feedback facilitation. Identifying how to increase the financial value of each client is one of the fastest and easiest ways to improve your business profit. You can read more about how to do this in Chapter 15, 'Creating your 360 products'.

Use organisational learning from 360° feedback to identify further work

A well-run 360° feedback project creates a lot of organisational intelligence in addition to the individual feedback reports. Make sure in the planning stage that you have agreed how you will feed this back to the organisation, as the evidenced outcomes are a great place to identify and ask for further work. Learn more about this in Chapter 15.

Invest in yourself and get help when you need it

One of the fastest ways to sabotage your success is to try to do everything yourself. To be successful you need to work with other experts, whether that means someone to stretch your thinking, to teach you a new skill or to help with the functioning of your business, such as administration or providing your online 360 platform. To be successful, you need to recognise when outsourcing will make a more appropriate use of your time, money and other resources. You also have to be prepared to invest in your own development and to identify what you need to learn in order to move your business forward, not just what you want to learn. Explore this further in Step 7 of the Success Mindset.

CHAPTER 15

Creating your 360 products

Using 360° feedback

As with all tools used in personal development, there are circumstances where 360° feedback is the ideal tool and circumstances where it is absolutely the wrong tool, as well as many areas where it is one of a number of interventions that will give clarity and direction. The main aim of any tool in personal development, particularly in work situations, is to enhance self-awareness, to improve interaction with others and to increase effectiveness. The results should focus on identifying potential, building individual talent and helping the individual to realise their goal or dream. Of course, in a corporate setting there is also an expectation that development interventions will identify the individual's specific strengths and development needs in their role, move them closer to work objectives and generally enhance their performance – in other words, make them better at what they do.

These two objectives, the personal and the organisational, can sometimes appear to conflict. An outcome that works for both the individual and the organisation is to use the 'best self' approach. Once the individual you are working with can identify and operate as the best version of him or herself, most of the time, things become easier and more enjoyable. This is rather like the personal excellence discussed in Step 5 of the Success Mindset. When you engage with the best version of yourself, you put more effort into success and performance and your outlook and mood will generally be more positive. For our clients, this translates into people – their team - who are more open and creative, more responsive to feedback and more engaged with what is going on around them. These people generally work harder, have less absence from work and stay in the organisation for longer. Those who can identify their best self also tend to display a greater sense of organisational citizenship. Dennis Organ demonstrates the value and advantages of high levels of organisational citizenship on performance in his research over the last two decades (Organ, Podsakoff and MacKenzie, 2006).

A significant part of project planning involves understanding why 360° feedback has been chosen and what the client (usually the organisation) is trying to achieve. It is worth considering the overall role of 360° feedback in isolation its own right, before applying it to a specific project. There are many benefits to using 360° feedback, as well as a great many myths about its function and implementation. It's worth busting a few of those myths (Box 15.1).

Box 15.1: The myths and reality of 360° feedback

Myth 1: Online 360 surveys are the feedback

Reality: 360 surveys are the data-collection and report-creation part of a bigger 360° feedback process.

Myth 2: 360 data is an accurate reflection of organisational performance

Reality: 360 data provides a subjective snapshot of individuals in the organisation, based on the questions asked.

Myth 3: 360° feedback creates positive change

Reality: 360° feedback is a tool; positive change is a process aided by 360° feedback and effective facilitation.

Myth 4: Benchmarking data improves the quality of the information

Reality: Benchmarking between organisations is meaningless; it is very unlikely that the data collected will compare like with like. The organisational culture, attitude to development and implementation process of the 360 project all create significant variables.

> **Myth 5 – Interpretation of 360 feedback results is easy**
>
> **Reality** - The feedback report should be straightforward and easy to understand; however it is the sharing of that information with the appraisee that takes the real skill. There are a number of factors affecting people's ability to be objective about their own feedback and an experienced facilitator will get a much better outcome than the report alone.
>
> **Myth 6 – Leaders improve after 360 feedback**
>
> **Reality** - This is a complex issue as there are many factors to consider, like the quality of feedback facilitation, the leader's commitment to make change, and his / her underlying personality. Research suggests most leaders do make some changes to behaviour, but without sustained support in the period after the 360° feedback most revert to behaviour patterns they are familiar and comfortable with.

None of these myths presents any great surprises, but they do help you to position the case for a fully facilitated project when you discuss successful 360° feedback interventions with potential clients.

It is also important to understand when 360° feedback is the best tool for your client to use. It is best for evaluating recent performance and communication, as well as for identifying talent and creating opportunities. 360° feedback is also good at identifying individual and organisational training/development needs. It also helps individuals to identify potential behavioural blocks to their progress.

It is not appropriate to use 360° feedback in place of performance management; where it is not relevant to or connected with organisational strategy; where it is directly linked to pay and rewards;

or where the organisational culture is not mature enough to handle the outcomes. It is also not advisable to undertake 360° feedback when there is no engagement in the process, either from seniors or from appraisees; or where there is no system to support the 360° feedback or no follow-up activity for participants.

Figure 15.1 shows how 360° feedback is used along the development–performance spectrum.

Figure 15.1: The development–performance spectrum

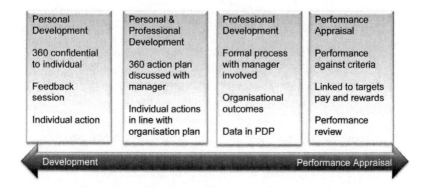

360° feedback on the development side of the spectrum often yields better results because it considers past, present and future behaviours. The appraisee can focus on how to change rather than just what to change. It is often both developmental and emotional, involving the appraisee and the organisation in partnership. In contrast, 360° feedback in performance reviews can be less effective. It is operationally based and focuses on past activity. It is led by the organisation and usually has consequences linked to pay, promotion and access to training. In these circumstances it can be more difficult to get honest engagement with the 360 process.

Whatever the primary reason for undertaking 360° feedback, it works best when it is aligned with organisational culture and reflects the values, competencies or goals of the organisation. Senior internal involvement and support are important for success, even when the project is being managed by an external coach or consultant.

Finally, whenever 360° feedback is used, either internally or with an external coach, it is critical that the project runs seamlessly for the appraisees and their respondents, therefore the coach must have a thorough knowledge of the tool he or she is using.

Running an effective 360° feedback project

There are four distinct stages to a successful 360° feedback project (Box 15.2). Each is important, and missing any out or partially completing one stage will jeopardise the success of your feedback intervention.

Box 15.2: Four feedback fundamentals

Stage 1: Planning
Stage 2: Information process
Stage 3: Feedback process
Stage 4: Organisational learning

All 360° feedback interventions require stage 2, and most people engage in some aspects of stage 3. It is surprising how many organisations launch into 360° feedback without any real consideration of stages 1 and 4. This makes a huge difference to the outcome of the project, the perceptions of those involved in the project and the perceived value of the intervention. As a coach or consultant selling 360° feedback you are well placed to take your client through this process systematically, in a way that gives them the best return on investment and that provides individual value to the participants. The four feedback fundamentals described below will take you through the process of an effective 360° feedback intervention.

Stage 1: Planning

There are two parts to the planning process; the first is about the clarity of the project and the second is about the practicalities of organisational engagement, ensuring that all of the people involved understand the hows, the whats and the wheres.

Be specific about the reasons for using 360° feedback

There are several different reasons why organisations choose to use 360° feedback. Clarity about the purpose of the 360 intervention, what your client is hoping to gain from the process and whether 360 is the right intervention for your client's desired outcome is critical.

As mentioned above, 360° feedback is best for supporting personal development and organisational growth. It offers a perspective on management and leadership skills that is difficult to get through any other method, and the very nature of feedback from real people who the appraisee actually works provides very powerful information about how they interact with different groups of people.

This type of intervention gives huge insights into an organisation's culture, values and priorities, all of which need to be considered when setting up your 360 project. It is critical that you discuss thoroughly with your client what their understanding is of the 360 process you are implementing, what information they would like to collect and what they intend to use it for. This will ensure that you use the right questionnaire and have prepared the appraisees and respondents in the appropriate way.

Case study 15: Clarity of purpose

Nigel, a development consultant working with the health sector, demonstrates the importance of clarity very well. On the face of it, he planned his 360 project carefully, asked the client what they were trying to achieve, and arranged a support package for appraisees and training for internal managers involved in facilitating feedback. His understanding from the HR director was that the 360° feedback was part of a leadership development package that was being run internally by the organisation. Each manager would attend a pre-360 briefing run by Nigel and then 360° feedback would be undertaken.

Nigel worked with me to design the questionnaire, sampled it with an HR manager and then rolled it out to the first cohort of

NHS managers. At the introductory briefing a number of issues and concerns were raised by the first cohort, about trust in particular, and about how the 360° feedback would be used. The last time some of that team had undertaken 360° feedback had been a destructive experience for them, with a heavy focus on negative feedback. Nigel was able to tell them with conviction that his understanding from the HR team was that the 360 project was purely for development purposes. This was well received and first cohort started their 360 data collection.

Nigel then ran some training for managers who would be involved in facilitating and supporting the managers to act on the outcomes of the 360° feedback. This was where his difficulty started. The managers had a completely different view of the purpose of the 360 project. They felt that it had replaced standard appraisal and individual performance review (IPR) and was different to the leadership programme. Nigel was unable to get clarity from the HR director, who now appeared to have changed his position on the purpose of 360° feedback.

With the briefing session for the second cohort looming, and a fair amount of non-participation from the first cohort, Nigel came to me for some support around how to proceed. He felt that he had been misled by the organisation, and didn't want to be complicit in misleading the next cohort. We discussed his position and his options and decided that he needed to discuss his position and ethical concerns with the HR director and decide a course of action to ensure that all parties had the same understanding of the purpose of 360° feedback.

This resulted in Nigel facilitating a meeting between the HR director, the senior managers and the appraisees. A lot of historical baggage and cultural misconceptions were discussed. It was agreed that the 360° feedback was a development tool and, as the questionnaire had been designed for development, that it would form part of the appraisal process, but that the appraisees' performance criteria linked to professional pay banding could not be measured from the 360° feedback. Nigel continued with the project, but throughout it he had to manage a high index of suspicion from both appraisees and respondents, which significantly slowed the progress of the intervention.

Nigel felt that his biggest learning experience was that he should have ensured that all parties understood the same purpose before he started; he would have approached the set-up meetings differently and he felt that the process would have been more open. In reality, Nigel had done a lot more to get the project right than many do. It is worth ensuring that you involve all stakeholders before the 360 project starts, if at all possible, and don't assume that the organisation has had those discussions already.

Organisational engagement

The prospect of having 360° feedback can be daunting, exciting and, for some people, extremely uncomfortable. Good planning increases organisational engagement, without which it is difficult for your 360 project to succeed.

It is critical that the participants, both appraisees and respondents, understand the whys, whats and whens of the 360 intervention. Good planning includes:

Box 15.3: Good planning for 360 projects

- Ensuring organisational awareness
- Dealing with fear and poor past experiences
- Choosing the right questionnaire
- Preparing participants
- Timing

Ensuring organisational awareness - If participants don't understand the reason why the 360 intervention is taking place they may not fully engage with it or may even attempt to sabotage it. Often managers setting up 360° feedback projects overlook this, assuming that employees know why the 360 project is taking place. Your role is to ensure that everyone involved understands the whys of the project.

Dealing with fear and poor past experiences - If the organisation or individual appraisees have had poor 360° feedback experiences in the past they need the opportunity to discuss this and gain confidence that your project will be different. Much of the concern revolves around confidentiality and people's interpretation of what that means. This is one area where you need to be unequivocal. To some extent it doesn't matter how much actual confidentiality there is in the project, provided that everyone involved understands the degree to which information is attributed to individual respondents or is shared within the organisation. What is important is that you understand the degree of confidentiality and anonymity, and that you can defend it.

Ideally, the project will be set up so that individual respondents cannot be identified and their names do not appear in feedback reports. The appraisee's understanding of the degree of confidentiality around who sees their report is also important. Take time to identify who will be facilitating the feedback, how it will be given and with whom the information will be shared.

Choosing the right questionnaire - The information that you get out of the 360 process will only be as good as the questions you ask. There are 'ready to go' 360 frameworks and these cover the areas commonly examined in the 360 process; however, one of the advantages of operating in a niche area is specialist expertise. This enables you to develop bespoke questionnaires to meet your clients' needs. This doesn't mean that you have to become a competency expert or spend hours reinventing the wheel. It does mean that you can use a library of existing 360 questions, edit them and create a questionnaire using language and behaviours relevant to your niche area. The Appraisal360 system allows you to develop multiple questionnaires and 360 frameworks for your own use, so you really can offer your clients a bespoke 360 package (Box 15.4).

Box 15.4: Characteristics of a good 360 questionnaire

- Questions should be relevant to the appraisee's role.
- The overall questionnaire should not be too long.
- Coverage will usually be fewer than 10 competency areas and around 7 questions per competency.
- Individual questions should be clear, short and ask only one question.
- Free text questions should be open ended.

Preparing participants - Both appraisees and respondents need to understand what is expected of them during the 360 process. Appraisees need to know how to access their 360, that they will need to complete a self-perception questionnaire and how to choose their respondents. They also need to understand what happens when the report is completed, what the report will be used for and what is expected of them. Choosing the right respondents is key to a meaningful 360 intervention. 360 projects are run in different ways, but it is usually best practice to enable the appraisee to choose their feedback respondents, or at the very least involve them in the choice. It is usually valuable to offer guidance about how many respondents to choose and what mix of people they should be. It is also important to give appraisees some information about choosing people whose opinions they value and who they can trust to give honest and constructive feedback – not just people who'll be nice.

Respondents also need some guidance on why the 360 project is being undertaken, why their honest feedback is needed and, most critically, what degree of confidentiality there will be. This can vary, depending on which respondent group they belong to. For example, an appraisee may have only one manager and it may be desirable to identify managers' feedback. Most 360° feedback is partially anonymised in that the names of the respondents are known to the appraisee although they are not included in the report and it is not possible for the appraisee to attribute feedback to a specific individual. Depending on how the 360 platform is used, it is possible to completely anonymise the report by removing rater groups and any colour coding associated with them.

Timing - Always allow more time than you think you need. The average 360 project takes around six weeks to get to the report stage. This allows for respondents being on leave, off sick, losing the email, etc. It's better to under-promise and over-deliver than the other way around. If you think the 360 project is slipping behind, identify this with your client early on and solicit their help in chasing up their employees to complete.

As with most projects, the key to success with 360° feedback is effective planning. It's worth spending time at this stage because it will pay dividends further into the project.

Stage 2: Information process

The information stage is the one part you can't have a 360° feedback without. An easy data-collection process and comprehensive but easy-to-understand report are the primary considerations of this phase.

Data collection

The key to this part of the process is to make it simple to implement, robust, secure, and easy to collate. In the belief that it will save money, coaches, as well as organisations, often get tempted to do this part themselves, using spreadsheets or survey software. This is a sure-fire way to create work and damage the success of your project. The time it takes to set up and administer the project and to collate the information will cancel any financial saving. I would always recommend using a good online supplier for ease, quality and ultimately, value.

A good online process is preferable to a software-based service because it is much easier for you and your clients to access. A web-based and email-driven process is easy for appraisees and respondents to use at their convenience. An example can be found at www.appraisal360.co.uk.

A good online process should include a means of overseeing and administering your 360 projects (Box 15.5). It should have a simple allocation process for distributing 360° feedback worksets to your appraisees and it should give you the opportunity to change respondents, send reminders and generate your reports when they are ready. For the appraisee, there should be a unique login, access to an overview of the progress of their 360, the opportunity to complete a self-perception questionnaire and a way to add respondents. A good online service will also provide a helpdesk facility for you, your appraisees and their respondents, should it be needed.

Box 15.5: A good online 360 process

For the coach
There should be a simple way to:

- Administer and oversee your 360 projects
- Allocate 360 appraisals
- Monitor progress and send reminders
- Add and remove respondents
- Generate feedback reports

For the appraisee
There should be a simple way to:

- Overview the progress of their own 360
- Complete their self-perception questionnaire
- Add or remove respondents
- Access their report when appropriate

A helpdesk facility should also be available for you, your appraisees and their respondents.

Feedback reports

A clear 360° feedback report is important for appraisee engagement. The report design and layout, as well as the actual feedback information, play a huge part in the effective understanding and use of the feedback (Box 15.6). Feedback reports need to be clear and make it easy to understand what the information is really telling you. Be wary of too many graphs, comparisons and averages, which can be misleading and may cloud actual feedback messages. Clear data with some method of triangulation enables both the appraisee and the feedback facilitator to get the most out of the report.

Box 15.6: The 360° feedback report

The report should include:

- A reminder of the scoring system and responder groups
- An overview of the whole 360° feedback, using average feedback from all respondents and average from self-perception
- Information about each competency in detail, giving actual scores from each respondent, colour coded into rater groups
- Free text information from respondents
- Highest and lowest-scoring behaviours

When using feedback reports produced by online 360° feedback providers, it is important to understand exactly what you are viewing. Always seek to get back the purest form of information possible. Many 360 providers have gone to great pains to create attractive reports that present simple information in graphical formats.

It's worth paying attention to what information you are actually getting and to be wary of too much averaging of feedback. When very small numbers are averaged, feedback findings can easily be skewed. For example, two raters in a group may produce an average score of 3, but the actual scores can have two completely different meanings when one is a 5 and the other a 1, as compared with two scores of 3. As a 360 project facilitator you will make the most use of actual scores from each respondent.

A good feedback report should be logical and intuitive, allowing you to work through it extracting information from competency areas and different responder groups and enabling you to use free-text comments to triangulate quantitative scores.

Figure 15.2: Sample of clear feedback report

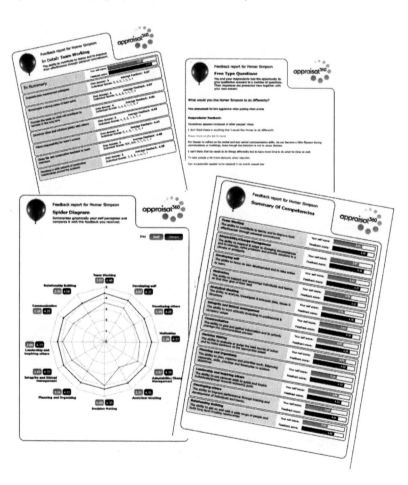

When you are facilitating someone else's feedback, interpreting the feedback reports can seem intimidating and it is worth undertaking some training with your chosen online provider to ensure that you get the best from the information in your appraisees' reports.

Stage 3: Feedback process

For the appraisee, this is the part of the process that makes the biggest difference. Managed well, it can help them to make significant shifts in perspective and behaviour. However, it is skilled facilitation that really makes the difference, not the information alone. Much research has been conducted around what type of feedback works best as a motivator and incentive for behaviour change. It is poor management of feedback that is responsible for many of the unsuccessful 360° feedback interventions. Negative feedback can be particularly destructive; while it increases the perceived urgency to change behaviour, it also decreases the belief that success is possible, by making any change seem more difficult. Part of the 360 facilitator's job is to reduce the perceived threat, build rapport and start to explore the feedback. You can make a profound difference to someone by using your excellent coaching skills to facilitate their understanding and acceptance of the feedback, therefore helping them to identify compelling actions as a result.

"The more threatening the feedback to the self, the more destructive it is."

Avi Kluger

An effective feedback session should focus on the positive first. Creating a positive emotional state enhances performance and a sense of empowerment, which in turn puts the appraisee in a better place to work with their feedback (Box 15.7).

Box 15.7: Strategies for effective feedback

- Share the report before the feedback session. In most cases, this enables the appraisee to move beyond their initial emotional reaction.
- Allow about an hour and half for a semi-structured feedback session, spending 30 minutes on the content of the report and the following hour on what the appraisee intends to do with the information.
- Use a workbook. This takes you through a series of exercises designed to create understanding. You can find an example of a workbook at http://www.appraisal360.co.uk/downloads.
- Focus on strengths. Small changes here can have a huge impact on performance.
- Development areas should be considered in two categories: allowable weaknesses and limiting weaknesses. Allowable weaknesses are those that have little relevance to the appraisee's role or well-being. It is probably not worth focusing too much attention on these. Limiting weaknesses are those areas that do impact on the appraisee's role, well-being or ability to do their job effectively, and these need to be addressed in the feedback meeting and development plan.
- Coach the appraisee to create compelling action plans. Use SMART type goals in action planning, as people recognise them and therefore it can be easier to use them.
- Ensure that there is a structure for follow-up, either through you or through someone in their organisation.

Stage 4: Identify organisational learning and areas for further work

One way to identify organisational learning is by collating the 360° feedback information to determine themes, organisational strengths and areas for development. Looking at individual feedback patterns will also allow you to identify those individuals at either end of the standard response curve, i.e. the high fliers and those who are underperforming. It may be that you will need to identify different or individual follow up interventions for these people.

This project overview will enable the organisation to focus training budgets on areas where they are most needed. So spend some time planning this and identifying where you can add further value. If you can offer a clear solution, you are in pole position for further work.

When reporting back to the organisation it is easy to get bogged down in detail. The key to success here is to stick to feedback headlines and themes, preferably in visual formats. This is your best opportunity to lay the foundations for further work, be clear about what you can offer and what further benefit it will have for the organisation and the individuals involved. If you can, include an identified cost benefit.

Whether or not you secure further work at the end of the 360 project, stay in touch with your client, continue to add value and keep the outcomes of the 360 project alive. This will ensure that you stay visible, so that you are the person the organisation thinks of first when they do have further development work. Ask for a recommendation, testimonial or referral, as this will continue to build your credibility and social proof.

Most people put a lot of time and emotional energy into their 360° feedback and, managed properly, it is a motivating, powerful and positive experience. Doing 360° feedback properly takes time, effort and care before, during and, most of all, after the data collection. This way the organisation gets proper return on its 360 investment. Effective 360° feedback projects do genuinely improve individual and organisational well-being, culture and performance. Follow the four fundamentals described here, and you will run successful feedback projects.

CHAPTER 16
Understanding sales strategy

The next two chapters are designed to help you with the sales process and to create a system that enables you to sell with ease. They look at how you engage with potential clients and how you ensure that you are invited to pitch for business. Chapter 16 gives you a system for sales meetings that takes away the pressure to pitch your product or service.

Building relationships

All interactions with potential clients – or prospects – should be seen as part of the sales process. From the very first interaction you or your company have with a prospect, you need to be sure that you make the impression you want to be remembered for. Selling your service or product is about relationship building, which is great news for the many coaches and trainers who hate the 'S' word (selling). It is only very, very late in the game that you engage in overt selling or asking for business – in fact, only once you are fairly sure that you have the deal.

"Stop selling, start helping."

Zig Ziglar

Your main role in the sales process is to get to know your prospect and create some value for them. Without building a relationship based on value you will not get the chance to actually sell anything. To ensure that you create the right relationship you first need to identify all the possible points of contact that your potential client has with you and your company. This includes your online presence – your social media (personal and company), your blog posts, your website, anywhere else they might find you through Google or other search engines. It includes any marketing you might do (either online or offline), your networking activity, public speaking and any opportunities they may have to see you or your employees/ associates in action.

People need to know you, as well as your company. In people development, whether clients are buying a service or a product, the human being at the other end of the sale is hugely important. Your clients want to like you, to be able to engage with you and either relate to you or aspire to be like you. Even more, they want to know that you relate to them – that you understand what they need and can provide it. To build an effective relationship, you need to ensure that every contact point for your potential clients moves them towards the solution or outcome they are looking for. This is much easier if you have worked out who your top clients are and what your topic/niche is, as outlined in Chapter 11 ('Know your niche').

The relationship-building phase can continue for a protracted period, particularly for high-cost purchases. Clients often ask me how long it takes to sell 360° feedback, or how many contacts a client needs before they buy, and the honest answer is 'it depends'. If you read the sales literature, time from introduction to sale can be anything between 7 and 21 points of contact. Part of the reason for this is the expanse of information now available to people, and part of it is that we may not always differentiate ourselves sufficiently from our competition. Active relationship building enables you to speed up the client's decision making by creating trust, by making the prospect feel that they know you and by being the person or company who can solve their problem.

There are six main reasons why people buy; understanding these and applying them to the pain or the wants of your client group will help you to ensure that your relationship building and contact points all feed into the end goal (Box 16.1).

Box 16.1: Reasons why people buy

- Fear of loss
- Comfort and convenience
- Desire for gain
- Security
- For ownership
- Emotional satisfaction

When creating points of contact with potential clients it's important to share some of your own story. Let people get to know you, get to like you and relate to or be inspired by you. If prospects feel that they know you and like you, they will want to support you and work with you because familiarity builds comfort – and when it comes to making big decisions, that reduces the perceived risk. At the end of the day, whether you are selling into large corporates or to individuals, you are selling to people. And people are most at ease with people they have some rapport with, who they trust and like. Those are the ones they buy from.

Influencing

Once you have started to build a relationship with potential clients and you have established some rapport through various contact points, even though you may not necessarily have met them you can begin to influence their decision-making process. Actively influencing other people should always be done with integrity and care, and, in my view, the sales process is no different. Managed properly, a good influencing strategy helps to move people to make a decision about an outcome they want (Box 16.2). Your challenge is to ensure you move them towards an outcome that you can provide better than anyone else; one that your client believes will genuinely help them; and one that will leave them a satisfied and loyal client. Everybody wins.

Box 16.2: Factors that create influence

- Commitment
- Difference
- Reciprocity
- Social proof
- Popularity
- Authority
- Legitimacy
- Scarcity

Commitment

Once someone makes a commitment to you, either by making a purchase, by investing their time in something you've created or by recommending something you've done, no matter what the cost in time and/or money, they will want to prove themselves right. This makes it a lot easier to move them down your sales funnel, providing you continue to meet their needs. People will buy more readily in the future once they have shown some small commitment. If you want to influence people to buy from you, make it easy by having plenty of access routes into your funnel and make sure that there are some low-cost commitment points.

Difference

People measure by comparing and contrasting what you provide with what your competitor provides. They then determine the value of what you are offering by comparing and contrasting this with their expectations. One of the key ways to influence decision making is to identify your differences and the value they bring to the client's situation. The key here is to stay real, to talk about things you can deliver and differences you can build on. The bigger the contrast you can create in key value areas, the greater the perceived attractiveness of your product or service.

Reciprocity

If you give something of perceived value to your potential client they are likely to want to give you something back. Make the most of this; ensure that anything you give away is something the client wants. In people development many people give away information, and while this is good and builds your credibility, remember also to stand out. Whatever you give away needs to reflect the value of the commitment you want to gain. For example, if you are at a conference and you want a bit of time to engage with potential clients, sweets, pens and branded items all buy you some time. If you want people to commit to a high-end project you may need to do something bigger, like an introductory training day. The key here is to look at where you are in the relationship-building process, identify what most helps your client to move to the next stage of their decision making, maybe it's dealing with their anxieties or handling possible objections, and then offer that solution for free. The majority of people will feel indebted to you if they have found your freebie of value.

Social proof

Trends influence decision making, so stay on top of what's happening in your industry, know what the press is saying and know what your competitors are doing. If something is topical or in the press, make sure that you are commenting on it, even if it's just a blog or an advice sheet to your mailing list. Although it is not always articulated, belonging is a fundamental human need. People want to feel part of a bigger cause, and they want the people they buy from to be part of a bigger cause too.

This same principle of belonging also applies to purchasing. If lots of people have something, others want it too. They like to feel connected. Use this to influence potential clients, extend corporate projects and create a community around what you offer. Online tools like 360° feedback, information products and membership sites are all good ways to do this.

Popularity

Familiarity increases your likeability factor – assuming that you are marketing yourself well. It also enables people to feel connected with you, to trust you and to be more responsive towards you. This in turn gives you a greater rapport; it makes your potential client more positively disposed to what you say and more easily influenced by you. Make sure that you let people get to know a bit about you and start to trust you; then use this area of influence with integrity – because if you breach that trust it will be hard to recover from it.

Authority

If you are considered an expert in your field, you are well known or your prospects perceive you to be an authority, they are more likely to be influenced by what you say. Make sure that your relationship-building activities position you in this way.

Legitimacy

This is about your boundaries. You want to be influencing your potential clients, not the other way around, so know what your negotiation limits are and stick to them. Be flexible with clients, but when they hit the boundaries tell them, and stick to your decision. Most clients will respect that; it raises your status and puts you in a better influencing position. Create policies if that helps; it can sometimes create a professional feel – for example, a cancellation policy for people who book events or coaching.

Scarcity

Another basic human characteristic: if there is not much of something left, everybody wants some before it's gone. Trade on this, again in a genuine way. You do have an inbuilt scarcity; there is only so much time in your diary, so treat yourself as a limited edition in short supply. People like to feel that they can have something special, that they got something others didn't, be it price, time, being first. Your value goes up with scarcity, so use it. If you sell a product that's not scarce and volume sales are what you want, e.g. digital information products or online 360, create the scarcity in a different way. Your clients will still build a relationship with you through your product, so use its uniqueness and special features to influence their decision making.

Understanding how to influence your clients' decision making is one of the best ways of increasing your selling potential. It will ensure that you get beyond the information transmission stage, into some real engagement – which in turn smoothes your access to actual sales meetings.

Excite your potential clients

We talked about passion a lot in Part 1. The sales process is where passion really pays dividends. If you are in rapport with your client, your emotional state will have an effect on them and it is most likely that some of your enthusiasm will be replicated in their own behaviour. To keep and use their excitement, make sure that you continually engage them. Use a variety of approaches and don't be afraid to be sensationalist, tie into what is topical or do something because it is amusing, just remember the core message still needs to resonate with their values and profile as discussed in Chapter 11 ('Know your niche'). Make sure that you know what matters to them and address it throughout the relationship building. Tell stories and create images in their mind, images that excite them about the solutions you offer, just like Dr Martin Luther King Jr did, (part 1), and make sure those images match with their values or beliefs . They will unconsciously associate themselves with your product or service and you will be able to guide their decision making. To get a successful outcome for both you and your potential client, you need to create synergy between what they want and what you are offering; understanding what excites them allows you to create compelling offers and calls to action.

Practise

Selling often feels daunting to people developers because it is often not a core skill that we learn. I believe that selling, like many things, is an unlearned behaviour; when we were small children we knew how to pitch our cause to get what we wanted; we sold ourselves to the other children when we first started school. Then gradually, as we gain different experiences, we remodel our behaviour and beliefs, based on those experiences and their perceived consequences. All of a sudden we don't know how to sell ourselves, our services, or our business anymore. Well, anything that can be unlearned can be relearned and with practice, behaviour can become familiar and comfortable.

I liken selling to riding a bike. When you first watch someone else ride a bike it seems easy. Then you have a go; it's not easy, in fact it's quite likely that you will fall off and bruise yourself. Then you might look a bit more closely at the actual actions needed to ride your bike, break down the parts and learn bit by bit. As you get back on and try, each time it gets a little smoother and the bits come together. Suddenly, if you pay attention to all the things you need to do, you can ride your bike. Now you've got it and you can keep going. Gradually you start to relax, to enjoy it even. You have become unconsciously competent. If you don't ride your bike for a while you still have the skills; you just need to dust them off and practise a bit.

The only real way to become good at selling is to practise, to know the component parts, to know your clients well and to know their pain points. Then perfect your story, how you position yourself and, most importantly, how you give the client the outcome they are looking for.

You should practise all the steps, not just what you will say at an important pitch. Practise and perfect the processes of understanding your clients, of building relationships, and of using influencing strategies ethically, then know how to excite people. You need to feel comfortable and passionate at a macro level, and be able to position your product or service in a way that engages your client group. Then you can move on to specific clients and individual sales pitches.

Reasons why sales don't close

Understanding the common reasons why people don't commit to purchasing helps to identify what to do to prevent this happening to you, as much as is possible (Box 16.3). All except number 5 are potentially avoidable if you find out enough about the client's specific wants before and during the sales meeting.

Box 16.3: Five reasons the client doesn't commit

1. There is no identified external pressure or compelling reason for the client to change.
2. The solution doesn't meet their pain points.
3. The perceived benefit is not enough or the return on investment has not been made clear.
4. The perceived risk is too great. There is not enough trust, rapport or social proof to do the deal.
5. The client is waiting to see other providers before committing.

Box 16.4 presents some common mistakes that coaches make when discussing new business with a potential client.

Box 16.4: Factors contributing to indecision by the client

1. **Failure to take the lead in the sales meeting**
   This can be done quite easily by setting some parameters at the beginning, like identifying the duration of the meeting or the desired outcome. It is about the coach, or sales person, identifying him / herself as an equal and managing the meeting.
2. **Not asking enough questions, then failing to understand the client's pain or drivers**
   It is very difficult to make a compelling offer if you don't really understand what the client is looking for, take time to ask questions and check your understanding.

---

3. **No compelling event or cost of not taking action**
   It is part of your role to outline the reasons for the client to take action. If you miss this opportunity you greatly reduce your likelihood of getting agreement to purchase.

4. **Chasing a big contract and missing the opportunity to get commitment to a smaller project first**
   It is tempting to always go for the high-value contract first, and sometimes that is right. It's also important that you stay focused on your client. If they're not going for your offer but are indicating a smaller purchase, take it – it's easier to sell to an existing client than to find a new one.

5. **Not bridging the gap between what the client wanted and the product or service offered**
   Sometimes this is as simple as going for the sale before you have found out enough about what the client wants and then getting it wrong. Often it is because the coach is fixated on what they have to offer and is not paying enough attention to what the client wants; hence, the product offered doesn't meet the client's needs.

CHAPTER 17

Managing the sales meeting

An effective strategy for managing sales meetings gives you confidence, allows you to relax and present yourself well and, most importantly, allows you to focus on your potential client and not on yourself.

Preparation

The real key to success is preparation. This is where knowing all you can about the client pays dividends. Understand what has got them to the meeting, what they want to achieve, all you can find out about the organisation, their culture and their decision-making processes. Most critically, identify where there are gaps in your understanding that need to be filled during the meeting. Know what you are offering before you go into the meeting. The wording and how you pitch can be formed during the meeting, but you must know your offer, where you have flexibility and where the boundaries are. This way, you look confident and in control – even if you don't feel it.

When selling into corporates, in particular, it is important to understand their buying process, to find out how many other providers they are meeting with (if any) and to see whether you can find out who these are. This helps you to prepare for the meeting and to know what your differences and selling points are.

Box 17.1: The key things to remember when preparing for the sales meeting:

- To be informed.
- To create some buyer urgency, while understanding the client's time-frame and processes.

- To create social proof, use case studies, reputation and understanding of the client's world.
- To appear flexible, understand what additional value the client is looking for and see where you can add this in, at little or no cost to yourself, to ensure that you get the deal.

The sales meeting

Coaches and people developers should be excellent sales people. The day of the oily salesman is long gone. Today's best sales are made by people who listen, question, and help the client to identify a course of action and then commit to it. Does this sound like a familiar strategy, and does it sound like a strategy you might actually be good at?

In sales, this technique is called the 'consultative sales method' (Figure 17.1).

Figure 17.1: The consultative sales method

Rapport ⟩ Listening ⟩ Asking questions ⟩ Assessment ⟩ Action ⟩ Close

The consultative sales method

Rapport

This is the number one essential component, without it you will find it very difficult to sell anything. By this stage, rapport is about reconnecting, building on trust, opening the door to conversation and understanding, and creating a safe environment for your client to share their desires, values and fears. Having rapport gives you a number of advantages; it allows you to pace your client, subtly match and mirror their behaviour, and lead them when appropriate. Using your sensory acuity helps you to judge where your client is in the decision-making process and take the necessary action. It is important that you maintain rapport throughout the sales process.

Listening and asking questions

The purpose of this phase is to find out as much as you can about how closely your client's wants, values and motives match your product or service. When you find out where you are at, you have the chance to close any potential gap during the conversation, rather than at the end of the meeting where you risk losing any deal. Use this phase to get the information you need so that you can make a compelling offer.

Listening well can make or break your sale. Active listening helps you to identify your client's motives, pain and wants in the language they use. It helps you to identify potential objections to the sale and to have a strategy to deal with these, and it allows you to reframe information about your product or service in a way that will be most helpful to your client. Listening also shows respect; it makes clients feel valued and important.

"You have two ears and one mouth – use them in proportion."

Sales training saying

One technique for staying focused on the sales conversation is to ensure that you know what you need to ask by planning in advance (Box 17.2). Then you will not be distracted from listening to your client by wondering what to ask next.

Box 17.2: What you need to find out

Listen for or ask about:

- Your client's pain
- The effect of the problem on them and what they perceive the solution to be
- What they would like instead of the problem
- What is most important to them
- How they recognise a good deal

Remember, this exercise is about your client, not about your product or service. You are seeking to understand, not to engage in pushy sales strategies. Use the meeting to tell the client what you offer by engaging in a conversation about their issues. Tell them how you can help them to achieve the outcome they are looking for.

Assessment

When you have explored all of the areas above you need to make a quick assessment of where you are at and how close your offering is to your client's wants; what objections to the sale you have identified; and how you can best meet the client's needs without compromising your position. While you are formulating your assessment and considering the next stage, it's worth checking where your client is at by asking them. Not only does this build the relationship further, it also enables you to tell whether you need to explore any objections to the sale in greater detail. Really drill down. Ask what specifically is not working and keep drilling down or asking in more detail, until you get to the issue. This will make a difference to the outcome of your sale. It will also give you the edge, because most people don't do it.

When you identify the obstacles to the client's solving their problem or achieving their goal, introduce ways in which you can help to solve it. Remain focused on what your service can do for them and how it can resolve their issue. Do not get tempted to delve into the features of your product, or the content of your course etc. Your client is not interested in them. They only want to buy an outcome!

It is likely that you will have identified some reasons not to buy during the conversation. If possible, reframe them, using stories and experiences from previous clients. Objections to buying are usually based in fear or lack (for example, lack of money, time, skill, self-belief) and can often be resolved by reframing the way the client looks at the problem. Being able to offer examples from others, or creating a success scenario, helps your client to stretch their thinking, imagine a bigger picture and often move past an objection relatively easily.

Case study 16: Mistrust

An NHS client of mine, a large hospital, had a problem with its leadership team in one clinical area. Senior management felt that the team were underperforming, that there were cliques within the team and two distinct groups who did not work with each other. This was affecting junior staff and the performance of the unit as a whole. The hospital wanted me to do some personality profiling and team building. I had discussed this at length and suggested 360° feedback, as opposed to a psychometric tool. I already knew that my client was unsure and had had a negative experience with 360 in another part of the hospital using a different provider a few years previously.

I went to the sales meeting armed with a case study of where 360 had worked well in very similar circumstances. I knew what my client's fears were and their mistrust of 360° feedback as a tool, but I was still convinced about its value in moving the clinical team forward. During the meeting we discussed what my client needed to do to manage the team's performance and what outcomes they needed from our intervention. I wove the methodology of my intervention into the conversation, without talking directly about 360° feedback. I focused on its outcomes, how it addressed team behaviour and brought individuals' behaviour under the spotlight, allowing a more constructive individual and team discussion to take place.

The hospital board was convinced that I had the solution, not because it was 360° feedback but because they trusted me;

I proved that I'd done it before and I talked about the things they were worried about and the safety nets we can put into the process. The intervention was carried out, together with a package of feedback and individual meetings followed by facilitated group work. The outcome for the hospital and the clinical team was one of improved relationships, improved productivity and a minor reshuffling of the leadership team.

Had I gone into the meeting to sell 360° feedback or teambuilding I would not have got the work. First I understood the complexity of my client's situation; then I convinced the hospital board that I could handle the team with sensitivity and compassion and still get the necessary outcome. And so my client trusted me.

A wise salesman, my father, once told me that someone always buys – either your client buys your product or you buy their excuses. If you go into a meeting prepared to deal with the common objections (Box 17.3), you should be able to manage the emotional responses to your conversation and lead your potential client to a different way of thinking and a more positive emotional place, using stories and case studies. The story allows them to dissociate from their fear or negative emotion and process the story, which, if chosen carefully and told well, will inspire them to take action.

Box 17.3: Common objections

- I don't have time.
- I don't believe you.
- I don't have the money.
- It won't work for me.

Part of your assessment is also about identifying real buying motives. Again, these are usually value driven and controlled by emotions. Once you have identified these it is much easier to frame your offer. This is much, much more powerful than any product attribute that you may be able to identify. Again, this will help you to move your client to take action.

Action

This is about getting your client to make a commitment. You need to know whether they are ready to buy, or where the conversation/ meeting goes from here. This is the point at which you need to test out options and fill in any gaps for them. You are looking to identify what else they might need in order to make a decision, before you make your compelling offer. Questions asked by sales teams typically include 'if I did this would you do that?' types of question, and some obvious 'yes' set questions to create a positive answer frame or to get the client in the habit of saying 'yes'.

A good way to keep the rapport and engage your client at this critical stage is to ask questions you know the answer to, usually about how the solution fits with their needs.

Case study 17: The solution that fits the need

A client bought the online 360 tool and couldn't make up his mind about the facilitation process. His objections were that the feedback might be too threatening for the directors, the directors might be too busy to travel for the feedback meeting and we might not be able to get it done in time for a big board away day. So I asked him if he saw the value of individual feedback. He said 'Yes'. I knew he would. I asked him if the directors would take their feedback better from someone external to the organisation. He said 'Yes'. Finally, I asked him whether, if I could put 360 facilitators into the key locations where the directors work and organise a meeting schedule for them, he would consider that workable. Again, he said 'Yes'. At that point I knew that we had a commitment to take action, so I closed the deal with an offer that ticked all of these boxes.

Closing the deal

This is the point at which you assume a sale, or commitment to action, and ask some option question relating to it, such as 'How would you like to pay?' If that is not appropriate, then 'When would you like to start?' or 'Do you have dates in mind?' If your client wavers at this stage, stay in rapport and wait. Some people need time and don't want to feel pressured. If they agree, agree terms with them and stop talking. *Many an experienced sales person has talked themselves out of a deal by not knowing when to stop.* Once you've made an agreement, move on to small talk – unless the client wants to talk about the detail of getting started.

This chapter and Chapter 16 have identified a structure for building relationships, using influencing skills with care and to help people make the right decisions. It has also identified a strategy for sales meetings that is not dissimilar to some of the strategies people developers use with their clients. It is this familiarity that should help you to prepare for sales meetings and get the best out of your potential clients.

Conclusion

A well-run, passion-driven business can truly set you free; it allows you to create the lifestyle that is right for you, to work the hours you choose and spend your time doing what you love – most of the time. This does not just happen because you have a dream, or a passion, and it is not just about technical skill in your chosen field. Building a successful business takes time, effort and focus, as well as a combination of business skills and the right mindset. Even with all of this, successful business owners get it wrong sometimes. We have a great marketing idea that flops, make the odd mistake in implementation or create a product the market hates. This is the road to success, and without trying different options you cannot move beyond your current place. Turnover might increase a little, business might become a little less challenging, but real success – your big dream – will elude you unless you are prepared to try different ways of thinking and acting. Successful business owners fail occasionally because they are pushing for more and trying different things; but because they move forward with persistent focus and the right mindset, these failures do not hold them back or knock them off course. They learn and move on, they don't get in their own way. This makes them stand out from the majority who dwell on what hasn't worked, either repeating the same behaviour or giving up.

This book has explored the Seven Steps needed for a Success Mindset. Being able to identify where your blocks are and to find strategies to manage or obliterate them will give you a fundamental shift of focus and attitude towards your business and your success. If you have completed the exercises in this book you have probably already identified some areas where you need to focus to realise your dreams and goals. Maintaining a Success Mindset requires work, up-front effort to determine what you want and effort along the way to ensure that you don't sabotage yourself. Most of all, the Success Mindset is a mindset that frees you to take action towards what you want, not one that keeps you trapped by your own thoughts. Following the Seven Steps and applying what you've read really will make a difference to your success.

Business skills are also important, and too many coaches fail because they don't have the required skill set. The process described in this book is a tried and tested formula, used by most successful businesses, regardless of industry. Knowing your client base intimately, knowing what differentiates you from others in your market and being able to position yourself as an expert makes success much, much easier. The time and effort that you spend applying the strategies described in this book will pay dividends and will enable you to stand out from the crowd.

When you do stand out, you need something to stand for, so make sure you have a clear sales funnel. Start at the bottom with a clear, high-profit product or service and work your way back up the funnel, always keeping your ideal client in mind. At the top of the funnel ensure that you have plenty of routes in – or, in other words, your ideal clients can find you easily and will clearly understand why you are the one with whom they should work.

The 360 Feedback Formula applies these principles and identifies how the use of a product can open doors for you, particularly when it is tailored to your client's desired outcome. The book describes how successful 360° feedback interventions are created and managed and how you can leverage further work from them. The 360 Feedback Formula shares a system successfully used to grow my own niche 360 business, Health Service 360.

If you want a successful business, you need a strategy to get clients buying from you. This is about building relationships, letting your potential clients get to know you and how you can help them. In people development overt selling is often unpopular. The easy solution is that if you are uncomfortable with it, don't do it. Your clients don't want to hear about your products anyway: they want solutions and outcomes for their own problems and desires. This book has shown you how to sell with ease, how to influence your clients and what pitfalls to avoid. With this information you can glide into sales meetings, consult with your client, listen to them, ask questions to assess where they are at, then excite them about possibilities and options and facilitate their decision to take action. These are skills that, as a people developer, you already have. Use them well.

One final thought. If you are still reading this book you have the persistence and commitment to succeed. If you apply what you have read, the process will make your journey much easier. If you've skipped straight to the conclusion, you may be really keen to succeed and to glean all the top tips from this book in a big hurry. You will have also missed the groundwork that makes the difference, the things that will make you stand out and the pitfalls that you need to avoid. Success requires planning, direction and focus as well as self-belief, stamina and resilience. Success also requires that you invest in yourself to ensure you have the right mindset and skill set – so read plenty, identify your role models, surround yourself with successful people who stretch your thinking, and work with the best mentors and coaches you can find.

The formula for business success has been laid out in this book. Use it and share it. The world needs people developers more than ever before and there is plenty of work to be had in the industry. Most people follow traditional business and marketing patterns. You can be different. You can stand out in a crowded market and have clients seeking you out, by following the strategies in this book. I wish you every success on your business journey.

References and further reading

CIPD (2011) 'Feedback-360 degree', www.cipd.co.uk/hr-resources/factsheets/360-degree-feedback.aspx

Edwards, M.R., Ewen, A.J. (1996) *360° feedback: The powerful new model for employee assessment and performance improvement.* New York: American Management Association.

Ericsson, A.K., Prietula, M.J. et al. (2007) 'The making of an expert', *Harvard Business Review,* 85(7–8), 114–21.

Gladwell, G. (2002) *Tipping point: How little things can make a big difference.* New York: Little, Brown and Company

Gladwell, G. (2007) *Blink: The power of thinking without thinking.* New York: Little, Brown and Company

Gladwell, G. (2011) *Outliers: The story of success.* New York: Little, Brown and Company

Godin, S. (2005) *Purple cow: Transform your business by being remarkable.* New York: Portfolio

Godin, S. (2008) *Tribes: We need you to lead us. New York: Portfolio*

Heath, D. and Heath, C. (2007) *Stick: Why some ideas survive while others die.* New York, Random House.

Hill, N. (1963, first published 1937) *Think and Grow Rich.* Chichester: Capstone Publishing.

Kluger, A.N. and DeNisi, A. (1996) 'The effects of feedback interventions on performance: A historical review, a meta-analysis, and a preliminary feedback intervention theory', *Psychological Bulletin,* 119(2), 254–84.

Likert, R. (1932) 'A technique for the measurement of attitudes', *Archives of Psychology,* 22(140), 55.

Morrison, P. (2011) *Virtuous and vicious circles: Getting the best out of 360 degree feedback*. Dusseldorf: VDM Verlag.

Organ, D.W., Podsakoff, P.M., MacKenzie, S.P. (2006) *Organizational citizenship behavior: Its nature, antecedents, and consequences*. London: Sage Publications.

Patterson, K., Grenny, J. et al. (2007) *Influencer: The power to change anything*. New York: McGraw Hill

Patterson, K., Grenny, J. et al. (2011) *Crucial conversations: Tools for talking when stakes are high*, 2nd edn. New York: McGraw Hill

Rock, D. and Page, L. (2011) *Coaching with the brain in mind: Foundations for practice.* Hoboken, NJ: John Wiley & Sons Inc.

Shipper, F. (2009) 'Investigating the sustainability of a sustained 360 process', *The 2009 Best Papers Proceedings of the Academy of Management Annual Meeting, Chicago, IL*. Academy of Management.

About Appraisal360

Appraisal360 is one of the UK's leading 360° feedback providers. It offers a robust, reliable online service that is fast, flexible and easy to use.

Whether you are running a large corporate project or just want to offer 360° feedback to an individual coaching client, the Appraisal360 system facilitates the administration of your projects; it collects and collates the data from your clients and produces attractive, comprehensive and easy-to-understand reports and workbooks to guide your feedback sessions. The system is flexible and allows you to run your projects in whatever way suits your clients' needs.

From the ground up, the 360 system has been built with the user in mind. Your clients won't be struggling with a badly designed system, or ringing you up every five minutes to find out what to do next. They will be using an intuitive, straightforward system that has worked well for thousands of people. And because the system is web based, your clients only need an email address and access to the internet to be able to use it.

If you have held back from using online 'tools' because you are not comfortable with the technology, you can relax secure in the knowledge that you are being backed up by experienced IT professionals with both the know-how and the infrastructure to ensure your success.

Appraisal360 has developed an industry leading 360 platform managed by Appraisal360's own internal software development team and technical support. It runs on dedicated enterprise-level servers and it is hosted at a high-security European data centre with off-site backup facilities. For security, there is an industrial-strength Cisco firewall, every login attempt is logged, there is a real-time email validation system and we encrypt all our questionnaire access links to prevent unauthorised access.

Safe in the knowledge that the underlying IT platform is taken care of for you, you can focus on getting the right 360 intervention for your client. You need to consider the degree of customisation you want, from ready-to-go frameworks to built from scratch bespoke questionnaires, you can even create your own questionnaires using the on line 'profiler' tool. If corporate branding is important to you or your client, Appraisal360 have the ability to create a fully branded 360 service to match the look and feel of your organisation. There are also a range of specialist analysis and management tools to help you get the best out of larger corporate projects; and to identify where there are opportunities for organisational learning and the potential for further work.

If you are new to using 360° feedback, want a refresher, or want to learn about advanced 360 techniques, the Appraisal360 Practitioner Network offers a range of training programmes as well as an Authorised Practitioner system where you can showcase yourself where our clients are looking for help with 360° feedback.

If you are planning on building a niche 360 product to serve a specific market sector, the Appraisal360 system has the tools, the online platform and the knowledge to support you. If you want to provide excellent service to your clients, to run your 360 projects with ease and have the peace of mind that the technology will work, then Appraisal360 delivers.

www.appraisal360.co.uk

appraisal360

What others say...

"Having run my own business for many years I was looking to set up a new company with a colleague, providing people solutions to the legal sector. I felt I knew what I was doing, but my colleague and I decided to attend Lynda's business development workshops to get a few tips and confirm that we were on the right track.

Lynda's approach was pragmatic and totally engaging having a profound effect on the way we approached our new business venture. I moved from '*I know all this but it won't work for me*' to '*This process has speeded up my thinking and got me into action*'

Her supportive but tenacious manner ensured that the whole group moved forward in developing our businesses enabling the group holding itself to account for progress."

Jane Green-Armytage, Athena Legal
www.athenalegal.co.uk

"I'm a bit of a seminar junkie, I enjoy them from a social perspective as well as for the learning, but before I met Lynda I suppose I was a bit stuck. Although I'd been to a lot of seminars and got lots of books, but I didn't do much with the things I learned. The first time I heard Lynda speak she made me feel a bit uncomfortable – like she could see inside my head, like she knew the real reasons I didn't do anything to grow my business. I knew if I worked with her she would challenge me, and not let me drift along and I was right. I don't just accept any healthcare consultancy I can get anymore; I have a niche – patient safety; I charge more than before, and I enjoy what I do. The difference is the clarity and focus about my consultancy business, and Lynda helped me get that."

David Adams, Adams Associates

"Lynda is expert in the design and delivery of 360 feedback and skilled at helping others to think strategically and creatively about the development of their own coaching and training business. Even better, she does this with enthusiasm, warmth and humour. I'm looking forward to working with her again"

Helen Hobart, Cornerstones Coaching
www.cornerstonescoaching.co.uk

"I joined Lynda's Business Development Programme at a time when I needed to refocus my business. It has been incredibly helpful and insightful, Lynda has a real gift for identifying the key issues and challenging you to marshal your thinking. I've already acted on many of the things I've learnt, with great success. I've really enjoyed the support and the content – Lynda is an expert in her field, it's been great to be able to share her experience. I'd recommend it to anyone who is serious about taking their business to a new level."

Julie Cooper, Spring Development
www.tsmpartnership.co.uk

"I have welcomed the knowledge and understanding that Lynda has of a wide range of business practices including business start-up, business development, marketing, internet promotion, selling at conferences and the way in which she can work with entrepreneurs in a conference situation or in a 1:1 mentoring situation. She is always willing to go the extra mile to help and support those who would benefit from her knowledge and skills."

Philip Cullen MBA, Owner, Solutions for Managers
Visiting Executive Fellow Henley Management College
www.philipcullen.com

"Remember, it's moments of action that make the difference - make yours count."

Lynda Holt

Notes

Notes

Notes

Notes